THE SPREAD OF
NUCLEAR WEAPONS:
A DEBATE

THE SPREAD OF
NUCLEAR WEAPONS:
A DEBATE

Scott D. Sagan
Kenneth N. Waltz

W. W. NORTON & COMPANY • NEW YORK/LONDON

Copyright © 1995 by W. W. Norton & Company
Printed in the United States of America

First Edition

Composition and layout by Roberta Flechner Graphics

Library of Congress Cataloging-in-Publication Data
Sagan, Scott Douglas.
    The spread of nuclear weapons: a debate
    Scott D. Sagan, Kenneth N. Waltz.-1st ed.
    p.   cm.
    Includes index.
    1. Nuclear weapons.   2. Arms race.   3. Nuclear nonproliferation.
I. Waltz, Kenneth Neal, 1924–.   II.   Title.
U264.S233   1995   355.02'17—dc20   94-24470

ISBN 0-393-03810-6 (cloth)
ISBN 0-393-96716-6 (paper)

W. W. Norton & Company, Inc., 500 Fifth Avenue, New York, N.Y. 10110
W. W. Norton & Company Ltd., 10 Coptic Street, London WC1A 1PU

5 6 7 8 9 0

Contents

Preface and Acknowledgments   vii

Chapter 1   MORE MAY BE BETTER
Kenneth N. Waltz   1

Chapter 2   MORE WILL BE WORSE
Scott D. Sagan   47

Chapter 3   WALTZ RESPONDS TO SAGAN
Kenneth N. Waltz   93

Chapter 4   SAGAN RESPONDS TO WALTZ
Scott D. Sagan   115

Endnotes   137

Index   155

Map   THE SPREAD OF NUCLEAR WEAPONS: 162
1945 TO THE PRESENT

PREFACE AND ACKNOWLEDGMENTS

This book is about one of today's most critical international issues: the spread of nuclear weapons. In each year of the early 1990s, another country grabbed the attention of the international community by appearing on the brink of nuclear weapons capability. In 1991, the Soviet Union collapsed and four new states—Russia, Ukraine, Belarus, and Kazakhstan—were "born nuclear," inheriting portions of the Soviet nuclear weapons arsenal. In 1991, after the Gulf War, we discovered that Iraq had been only two years or so away from making atomic bombs, before the Desert Storm attack and the subsequent dismantlement by international inspectors of their weapons development facilities. In 1992, Pakistani officials admitted that they had developed a nuclear weapons capability, after over two decades of dedicated effort. In 1993, the South African government acknowledged that it had constructed a small nuclear arsenal in the 1980s, but said that it had dismantled and destroyed its weapons. North Korea was in the headlines in 1994, when the Pyongyang government refused to permit full international inspection of its nuclear facilities and the CIA presented the White House with its estimate that North Korea had processed enough plutonium for one or more bombs. What will come next? Other potential nuclear powers appear on the horizon: leading Japanese politicians no longer rule out acquisition of nuclear weapons and a growing number of developing nations, such as Iran, Libya, and Algeria, seem to have nuclear weapons programs.

This book is neither about who will get the bomb next nor about the technical and political processes by which states may develop nuclear weapons. There are plenty of books and government reports on these subjects. The purpose of this book is to address a more fundamental question: What are the likely consequences of the spread of nuclear weapons?

The answer is by no means certain or simple. Indeed, as readers will discover, we disagree about that central issue. Kenneth Waltz argues that fear of the spread of nuclear weapons is exaggerated: "More may be better" since new nuclear states will use their weapons to deter other countries from attacking them. Scott Sagan argues that the spread of nuclear weapons will make the world less stable: "More will be worse" since some new nuclear states will engage in preventive wars, fail to build survivable forces, or have serious nuclear weapons accidents.

In the first two chapters, we present our arguments and develop the logic and evidence that support each argument. In the third and fourth chapters we respond to each other's criticisms, showing where, on occasion, there is common ground and where, more often, strong disagreements remain.

Disagreements will take up much of this book. Here we point out some important matters of agreement between us. First, both of us believe that theories are a necessary aid to understanding international politics. Some may claim to present "just the facts" or to judge situations purely on "a case by case basis." Most individuals still have theories that guide their views, however, although they may not be well developed or clearly presented. We have both tried to lay out the assumptions and logic behind our positions and to show how these concepts can provide insights into problems of nuclear proliferation.

Second, both of us believe that intellectual debates are useful. We believe that ideas are improved through debate and through testing ideas against evidence. We have found this debate to be stimulating and hope that those who read this book find that it serves a useful purpose.

Third, we believe that political scientists play a role in improving governmental policy. We study international politics because we believe it matters and that it influences all of our lives. We also write about international politics because we believe that scholarly writing has some influence on governments. By training and inclination, scholars are not well equipped to comment on the details of policy. Yet scholars do have critical roles to play in shaping policies by challenging underlying beliefs.

ACKNOWLEDGMENTS

First and foremost, we thank our wives, Sujitpan Bao Lamsam and Huddie Waltz, for enriching our lives and improving our work. We thank Roby Harrington for encouraging us to pit our ideas against one another and for serving as an editor with a light and talented touch. We would also like to thank Margie Brassil for her excellent work as our copy editor. Kenneth Waltz thanks the Institute for Global Cooperation and Conflict of the University of California for its continuing support, Karen Ruth Adams for her intellectual counsel, and Sandra Escobedo for research assistance. Scott Sagan thanks Stanford University's Center for International Security and Arms Control, the Carnegie Corporation of New York, the W. Alton Jones Foundation and the Peter Kiewit Foundation for their support, and Effie Toshav and Kevin Paige for their help as research assistants.

Finally, we want to thank our many students and colleagues whose comments on our work have improved our thinking on this subject and prevented us from making unnecessary mistakes. All remaining errors in the book, of course, are the fault of the other author.

Scott D. Sagan
Palo Alto, CA

Kenneth N. Waltz
Berkeley, CA

THE SPREAD OF
NUCLEAR WEAPONS:
A DEBATE

Chapter 1

MORE MAY BE BETTER

Kenneth N. Waltz

What will the spread of nuclear weapons do to the world? I say "spread" rather than "proliferation" because so far nuclear weapons have proliferated only vertically as the major nuclear powers have added to their arsenals. Horizontally, they have spread slowly across countries, and the pace is not likely to change much. Short-term candidates for the nuclear club are not numerous, and they are not likely to rush into the nuclear business. One reason is that the United States works with some effect to keep countries from doing that.

Nuclear weapons will nevertheless spread, with a new member occasionally joining the club. Membership grew to twelve in the first fifty years of the nuclear age, and that number includes three countries who suddenly found themselves in the nuclear military business as successor states to the Soviet Union. A 50 percent growth of membership in the next decade would be surprising. Since rapid changes in international conditions can be unsettling, the slowness of the spread of nuclear weap-

This is a revised version of my "Toward Nuclear Peace," in D. Brito and M. Intrilligator, eds., *Strategies for Managing Nuclear Proliferation* (Lexington, MA: Lexington Books, 1982) and *The Spread of Nuclear Weapons: More May Be Better*, Adelphi Paper 171 (London: International Instutute for Strategic Studies, 1981).

ons is fortunate. Someday the world will be populated by fifteen or eighteen nuclear-weapon states (hereafter referred to as nuclear states). What the further spread of nuclear weapons will do to the world is therefore a compelling question.

THE MILITARY LOGIC OF SELF-HELP SYSTEMS

The world has enjoyed more years of peace since 1945 than had been known in modern history, if peace is defined as the absence of general war among the major states of the world. The Second World War followed the first one within twenty-one years. Fifty years have elapsed since the Allies' victory over the Axis powers. Conflict marks all human affairs. In the past half century, conflict has generated hostility among states and has at times issued in violence among the weaker and smaller ones. Even though the more powerful states of the world were occasionally direct participants, war was confined geographically and limited militarily. Remarkably, general war was avoided in a period of rapid and far-reaching change: decolonization; the rapid economic growth of some states; the formation, tightening, and eventual loosening of blocs; the development of new technologies, and the emergence of new strategies for fighting guerrilla wars and deterring nuclear ones. The prevalence of peace, together with the fighting of circumscribed wars, indicates a high ability of the postwar international system to absorb changes and to contain conflicts and hostility.

Presumably, features found in the postwar system that were not present earlier account for the world's recent good fortune. The biggest changes in the postwar world were the shift from multipolarity to bipolarity and the introduction of nuclear weapons. In this chapter I concentrate on the latter.

States coexist in a condition of anarchy. Self-help is the principle of action in an anarchic order, and the most important way in which states must help themselves is by providing for their own security. Therefore, in weighing the chances for peace, the first questions to ask are questions about the ends for which states use force and about the strategies and weapons they employ. The chances of peace rise if states can achieve their most important ends without using force. War becomes less likely as the costs of war rise in relation to possible gains. Strategies bring ends and means together. How nuclear weapons affect the chances for peace is seen by examining the different implications of defense and deterrence.

How can one state dissuade another state from attacking? In either or in some combination of two ways. One way to counter an intended attack is to build fortifications and to muster forces that look forbiddingly strong. To build defenses so patently strong that no one will try to destroy or overcome them would make international life perfectly tranquil. I call this the defensive ideal. The other way to counter an intended attack is to build retaliatory forces able to threaten unacceptable punishment upon a would-be aggressor. "To deter" literally means to stop people from doing something by frightening them. In contrast to dissuasion by defense, dissuasion by deterrence operates by frightening a state out of attacking, not because of the difficulty of launching an attack and carrying it home, but because the expected reaction of the opponent may result in one's own severe punishment. Defense and deterrence are often confused. One used to hear statements like this: "A strong defense in Europe will deter a Soviet attack." What was meant was that a strong defense would dissuade the Soviet Union from attacking. Deterrence is achieved not through the ability to defend but through the ability to punish. Purely deterrent forces provide no defense. The message of the strategy is this: "Although we are defenseless, if you attack we may punish you to an extent that more than cancels your gains." Second-strike nuclear forces serve that kind of strategy. Purely defensive forces provide no deterrence. They offer no means of punishment. The message of the strategy is this: "Although we cannot strike back at you, you will find our defenses so difficult to overcome that you will dash yourself to pieces against them." The Maginot Line was to serve that kind of strategy.

Do nuclear weapons increase or decrease the chances of war? The answer depends on whether nuclear weapons permit and encourage states to deploy forces in ways that make the active use of force more or less likely and in ways that promise to be more or less destructive. If nuclear weapons make the offense more effective and the blackmailer's threat more compelling, then nuclear weapons are bad for the world—the more so the more widely diffused nuclear weapons become. If defense and deterrence are made easier and more reliable by the spread of nuclear weapons, we may expect the opposite result. To maintain their security, states must rely on the means they can generate and the arrangements they can make for themselves. It follows that the quality of international life varies with the ease or the difficulty states experience in making themselves secure.

Weapons and strategies change the situation of states in ways that make them more or less secure, as Robert Jervis has clearly shown.[1] If weapons are not well suited for conquest, neighbors have more peace of mind. We should expect war to become less likely when weaponry is such as to make conquest more difficult, to discourage preemptive and preventive war, and to make coercive threats less credible. Do nuclear weapons have those effects? Some answers can be found by considering how nuclear deterrence and nuclear defense improve the prospects for peace.

First, war can be fought in the face of deterrent threats, but the higher the stakes and the closer a country moves toward winning them, the more surely that country invites retaliation and risks its own destruction. States are not likely to run major risks for minor gains. War between nuclear states may escalate as the loser uses larger and larger warheads. Fearing that, states will want to draw back. Not escalation but deescalation becomes likely. War remains possible, but victory in war is too dangerous to fight for. If states can score only small gains, because large ones risk retaliation, they have little incentive to fight.

Second, states act with less care if the expected costs of war are low and with more care if they are high. In 1853 and 1854 Britain and France expected to win an easy victory if they went to war against Russia. Prestige abroad and political popularity at home would be gained, if not much else. The vagueness of their expectations was matched by the carelessness of their actions. In blundering into the Crimean War, they acted hastily on scant information, pandered to their people's frenzy for war, showed more concern for an ally's whim than for the adversary's situation, failed to specify the changes in behavior that threats were supposed to bring, and inclined toward testing strength first and bargaining second.[2] In sharp contrast, the presence of nuclear weapons makes states exceedingly cautious. Think of Kennedy and Khrushchev in the Cuban missile crisis. Why fight if you can't win much and might lose everything?

Third, the question demands an affirmative answer all the more insistently since the deterrent deployment of nuclear weapons contributes more to a country's security than does conquest of territory. A country with a deterrent strategy does not need the extent of territory required by a country relying on conventional defense. A deterrent strategy makes it unnecessary for a country to

fight for the sake of increasing its security, and this removes a major cause of war.[3]

Fourth, deterrent effect depends both on capabilities
and on the will to use them. The will of the attacked,
striving to preserve its own territory, can be presumed to
be stronger than the will of the attacker, striving to an-
nex someone else's territory. Knowing this, the would-be
attacker is further inhibited.[4]

Certainty about the relative strength of adversaries
also makes war less likely. From the late nineteenth century onward, the speed of technological innovation increased the difficulty of estimating relative strengths and
predicting the course of campaigns. Since World War II,
technological advance has been even faster, but short of
a ballistic missile defense breakthrough, this has not mattered. It did not disturb the American-Soviet military
equilibrium, because one side's missiles were not made
obsolete by improvements in the other side's missiles. In
1906, the British Dreadnought, with the greater range
and fire power of its guns, made older battleships obsolete. This does not happen to missiles. As Bernard Brodie put it, "Weapons that do not have to fight their like
do not become useless because of the advent of newer
and superior types."[5] They may have to survive their
like, but that is a much simpler problem to solve.

Many wars might have been avoided had their outcomes been foreseen. "To be sure," Georg Simmel wrote,
"the most effective presupposition for preventing struggle, the exact knowledge of the comparative strength of
the two parties, is very often only to be obtained by the
actual fighting out of the conflict."[6] Miscalculation causes
wars. One side expects victory at an affordable price,
while the other side hopes to avoid defeat. Here the differences between conventional and nuclear worlds are
fundamental. In the former, states are too often tempted
to act on advantages that are wishfully discerned and
narrowly calculated. In 1914, neither Germany nor

France tried very hard to avoid a general war. Both hoped for victory even though they believed the opposing coalitions to be quite evenly matched. In 1941, Japan, in attacking the United States, could hope for victory only if a series of events that were possible but unlikely took place. Japan hoped to grab resources sufficient for continuing its war against China and then to dig in to defend a limited perimeter. Meanwhile, the United States and Britain would have to deal with Germany, supposedly having defeated the Soviet Union and therefore supreme in Europe. Japan could then hope to fight a defensive war for a year or two until America, her purpose weakened, became willing to make a compromise peace in Asia.[7]

Countries more readily run the risks of war when defeat, if it comes, is distant and is expected to bring only limited damage. Given such expectations, leaders do not have to be crazy to sound the trumpet and urge their people to be bold and courageous in the pursuit of victory. The outcome of battles and the course of campaigns are hard to foresee because so many things affect them. Predicting the result of conventional wars has proved difficult.

Uncertainty about outcomes does not work decisively against the fighting of wars in conventional worlds. Countries armed with conventional weapons go to war knowing that even in defeat their suffering will be limited. Calculations about nuclear war are differently made. A nuclear world calls for a different kind of reasoning. If countries armed with nuclear weapons go to war, they do so knowing that their suffering may be unlimited. Of course, it also may not be, but that is not the kind of uncertainty that encourages anyone to use force. In a conventional world, one is uncertain about winning or losing. In a nuclear world, one is uncertain about surviving or being annihilated. If force is used, and not kept within limits, catastrophe will result. That prediction is easy to make because it does not require close estimates of opposing forces. The number of one's cities that can be severely damaged is equal to the number of strategic warheads an adversary can deliver. Variations of number mean little within wide ranges. The expected effect of the deterrent achieves an easy clarity because wide margins of error in estimates of the damage one may suffer do not matter. Do we expect to lose one city or two, two cities or ten? When these are the pertinent questions, we stop thinking about running risks and start worrying about how to avoid them. In a conventional world, deterrent threats are ineffective because the damage threatened is distant, limited, and problematic. Nuclear weapons make military miscalculation difficult and politically pertinent prediction easy.

WHAT WILL THE SPREAD OF NUCLEAR WEAPONS DO TO THE WORLD?

Contemplating the nuclear past gives ground for hoping that the world will survive if further nuclear powers join today's dozen. This hope is called into question by those who believe that the infirmities of some new nuclear states and the delicacy of their nuclear forces will work against the preservation of peace and for the fighting of nuclear wars. The likelihood of avoiding destruction as more states become members of the nuclear club is often coupled with the question of *who* those states will be. What are the likely differences in situation and behavior of new as compared to old nuclear powers?

Nuclear Weapons and Domestic Stability

What are the principal worries? Because of the importance of controlling nuclear weapons—of keeping them firmly in the hands of reliable officials—rulers of nuclear states may become more authoritarian and ever more given to secrecy. Moreover, some potential nuclear states are not politically strong and stable enough to ensure control of the weapons and control of the decision to use them. If neighboring, hostile, unstable states are armed with nuclear weapons, each will fear attack by the other. Feelings of insecurity may lead to arms races that subordinate civil needs to military necessities. Fears are compounded by the danger of internal coups, in which the control of nuclear weapons may be the main object of struggle and the key to political power. Under these fearful circumstances, to maintain governmental authority and civil order may be impossible. The legitimacy of the state and the loyalty of its citizenry may dissolve because the state is no longer thought to be capable of maintaining external security and internal order. The first fear is that states become tyrannical; the second, that they lose control. Both fears may be realized either in different states or in the same state at different times.[8]

What can one say? Four things primarily. First, possession of nuclear weapons may slow arms races down, rather than speed them up, a possibility considered later. Second, for less-developed countries to build nuclear arsenals requires a long lead time. Nuclear power and nuclear weapons programs require administrative and technical teams able to formulate and sustain programs of considerable cost that pay off only in the long run. The more unstable a government, the shorter becomes the attention span of its leaders. They have to deal with today's problems and hope for the best tomorrow.[9] In countries where political control is most difficult to maintain, governments are least likely to initiate nuclear-weapons programs. In such states, soldiers help to maintain leaders in power or try to overthrow them. For those purposes nuclear weapons are not useful. Soldiers who have political clout, or want it, are not interested in nuclear weapons. They are not scientists or technicians.

They like to command troops and squadrons. Their vested interests are in the military's traditional trappings.

Third, although highly unstable states are unlikely to initiate nuclear projects, such projects, begun in stable times, may continue through periods of political turmoil and succeed in producing nuclear weapons. A nuclear state may be unstable or may become so. But what is hard to comprehend is why, in an internal struggle for power, the contenders would start using nuclear weapons. Who would they aim at? How would they use them as instruments for maintaining or gaining control? I see little more reason to fear that one faction or another in a less-developed country will fire atomic weapons in a struggle for political power than that they will be used in a crisis of succession. One or another nuclear state will experience uncertainty of succession, fierce struggles for power, and instability of regime. Those who fear the worst have not shown how those events might lead to the use of nuclear weapons. Strikingly, during the Cultural Revolution, which lasted from 1966 to 1976, some group managed to keep control of China's nuclear weapons. Fourth, the possibility of one side in a civil war firing a nuclear warhead at its opponent's stronghold nevertheless remains. Such an act would produce a national tragedy, not an international one. This question then arises: Once the weapon is fired, what happens next? The domestic use of nuclear weapons is, of all the uses imaginable, least likely to lead to escalation and to global tragedy.

Nuclear Weapons and Regional Stability

Nuclear weapons are not likely to be used at home. Are they likely to be used abroad? As nuclear weapons spread, what new causes may bring effects different from, and worse than, those known earlier in the nuclear age? This section considers five ways in which the new world is expected to differ from the old and then examines the prospects for, and the consequences of, new nuclear states using their weapons for blackmail or for fighting offensive wars.

In what ways may the actions and interactions of new nuclear states differ from those of old nuclear powers? First, new nuclear states may come in hostile pairs and share a common border. Where states are bitter enemies one may fear that they will be unable to resist using their nuclear weapons against each other. This is a worry about the future that the past does not disclose. The Soviet Union and the United States, and the Soviet Union and China, were hostile enough; and the latter pair shared a long border. Nuclear weapons caused China and the Soviet Union to deal cautiously with each other. But bitterness among some potential nuclear states, so it is said, exceeds that felt by the old ones. Playing down the bitterness sometimes felt by the United States, the Soviet Union, and China requires a creative reading of history. Moreover, those who believe that bitterness causes wars assume a close association that is seldom found between bitterness among nations and their willingness to run high risks.

Second, many fear that states that are radical at home will recklessly use their nuclear weapons in pursuit of revolutionary ends abroad. States that are radical at home, however, may not be radical abroad. Few states have been radical in the conduct of their foreign policy, and fewer have remained so for long. Think of the Soviet Union and the People's Republic of China. States coexist in a competitive arena. The pressures of competition cause them to behave in ways that make the threats they face manageable, in ways that enable them to get along. States can remain radical in foreign policy only if they are overwhelmingly strong—as none of the new nuclear states will be—or if their acts fall short of damaging vital interests of other nuclear powers. States that acquire nuclear weapons will not be regarded with indifference. States that want to be freewheelers have to stay out of the nuclear business. A nuclear Libya, for example, would have to show caution, even in rhetoric, lest it suffer retaliation in response to someone else's anonymous attack on a third state. That state, ignorant of who attacked, might claim that its intelligence agents had identified Libya as the culprit and take the opportunity to silence it by striking a heavy conventional blow. Nuclear weapons induce caution in any state, especially in weak ones.

Third, some new nuclear states may have governments and societies that are not well rooted. If a country is a loose collection of hostile tribes, if its leaders form a thin veneer atop a people partly nomadic and with an authoritarian history, its rulers may be freer of constraints than, and have different values from, those who rule older and more fully developed polities. Idi Amin and Muammar el-Qaddafi fit these categories, and they were favorite examples of the kinds of rulers who supposedly could not be trusted to manage nuclear weapons responsibly. Despite wild rhetoric aimed at foreigners, however, both of these "irrational" rulers became cautious and modest when punitive actions against them might have threatened their ability to rule. Even though Amin lustily slaughtered members of tribes he disliked, he quickly stopped goading Britain when it seemed that it might intervene militarily. Qaddafi has shown similar restraint. He and Anwar Sadat were openly hostile. In July of 1977, both launched commando attacks and air raids, including two large air strikes by Egypt on Libya's el Adem airbase. Neither side let the attacks get out of hand. Qaddafi showed himself to be forbearing and amenable to mediation by other Arab leaders. Shai Feldman used these and other examples to argue that Arab leaders are deterred from taking inordinate risks, not because they engage in intricate rational calculations but simply because they, like other rulers, are "sensitive to costs."[10] Saddam Hussein further illustrated the point during, and even prior to, the war of 1991. He invaded Kuwait only after the United States had given many indications that it would not oppose him or use military force to liberate a Kuwait conquered by Iraq. During the war, he launched missiles against Israel. But Iraq's missiles were so lightly armed that little risk was run of prompting attacks more punishing than what Iraq was already suffering. Deterrence worked for the United States and for Israel as it has for every other nuclear state.

Many Westerners write fearfully about a future in which Third World countries have nuclear weapons. They seem to view their people in the old imperial manner as "lesser breeds without the law." As ever with ethnocentric views, speculation takes the place of evidence. How do we know that a nuclear-armed and newly hostile Egypt, or a nuclear-armed and still-hostile Syria, would not strike to destroy Israel? Would either do so at the risk of Israeli bombs falling on some of their cities? Almost a quarter of Egypt's people live in four cities: Cairo, Alexandria, El-Giza, and Shoubra el-Kheima. More than a quarter of Syria's live in three: Damascus, Aleppo, and Homs.[11] What government would risk sudden losses of such proportion, or indeed of much lesser proportion? Rulers want to have a country that they can continue to rule. Some Arab country might wish that some other Arab country would risk its own destruction for the sake of destroying Israel, but why would one think that any country would be willing to do so? Despite ample bitterness, Israelis and Arabs have limited their wars and accepted constraints placed on them by others. Arabs did not marshal their resources and make an all-out effort to destroy Israel in the years before Israel could strike back with nuclear warheads. We cannot expect countries to risk more in the presence of nuclear weapons than they did in their absence.

Fourth, while some worry about nuclear states coming in hostile pairs, others worry that they won't come in hostile pairs. The simplicity of relations that obtains when one party has to concentrate its worry on only one other, and the ease of calculating forces and estimating the dangers they pose, may be lost. Early in the Cold War, the United States deterred the Soviet Union, and in due course, the Soviet Union deterred the United States. As soon as additional states joined the nuclear club, however, the question of who deterred whom could no longer be easily answered. The Soviet Union had to worry lest a move made in Europe might cause France and Britain to retaliate, thus possibly setting off American forces as well. Such worries at once complicated calculations and strengthened deterrence. Somebody might have retaliated, and that was all a would-be attacker needed to know. Nuclear weapons restore the clarity and simplicity lost as bipolar situations are replaced by multipolar ones.

Fifth, in some of the new nuclear states, civil control of the military may be shaky. Nuclear weapons may fall into the hands of military officers more inclined than civilians are to put them to offensive use. This again is an old worry. I can see no reason to think that civil control of the military was secure in the Soviet Union, given the occasional presence of military officers in the Politburo and some known and some surmised instances of military intervention in civil affairs at critical times.[12] In the People's Republic of China, military and civil branches of government are not separated but fused. Although one may prefer civil control, preventing a highly destructive war does not require it. What is required is that decisions be made that keep destruction within bounds, whether decisions are made by civilians or soldiers. Soldiers may be more cautious than civilians.[13] Generals and admirals do not like uncertainty, and they do not lack patriotism. They do not like to fight conventional wars under unfamiliar conditions. The offensive use of nuclear weapons multiplies uncertainties. Nobody knows what a nuclear battlefield would look like, and nobody knows what will happen after the first city is hit. *Uncertainty* about the course that a nuclear war might follow, along with the *certainty* that destruction can be immense, strongly inhibits the first use of nuclear weapons.

Examining the supposedly unfortunate characteristics of new nuclear states removes some of one's worries. One wonders why their civil and military leaders should be less interested in avoiding their own destruction than leaders of other states have been.[14] Nuclear weapons have never been used in a world in which two or more states had them. Still, one's feeling that something awful will emerge as new nuclear powers are added to the present group is not easily quieted. The fear remains that one state or another will fire its new nuclear weapons in a coolly calculated preemptive strike, or fire them in a moment of panic, or use them to launch a preventive war. These possibilities are examined in the next section. Nuclear weapons, so it is feared, may also be set off anonymously, or used to back a policy of blackmail, or be used in a combined conventional-nuclear attack.

Some have feared that a radical Arab state might fire a nuclear warhead anonymously at an Israeli city in order to block a peace settlement.[15] But the state firing the warhead could not be certain of remaining unidentified. Even if a country's leaders persuaded themselves that chances of retaliation were low, who would run the risk? Nor would blackmail be easy, despite one instance of seeming success. In 1953, the Soviet Union and China may have been convinced by President Dwight D. Eisenhower and Secretary of State John Foster Dulles that they would widen the Korean war and raise the level of violence by using nuclear weapons if a settlement were not reached. In Korea, we had gone so far that the threat to go farther was plausible. The blackmailer's threat is not a cheap way of working one's will. The threat is simply incredible unless a considerable investment has already been made. On January 12, 1954, Dulles gave a speech that seemed to threaten massive retaliation in response to bothersome actions by others, but the successful siege of Dien Bien Phu by Ho Chi Minh's forces in the spring of that year showed the limitations of such threats. Capabilities foster policies that employ them. Using American nuclear weapons to force the lifting of the siege was discussed in both the United States and France. But using nuclear weapons to serve distant and doubtful interests would have been a monstrous policy, too horrible, when contemplated, to carry through. Nuclear weapons deter adversaries from attacking one's vital, and not one's minor, interests.

Although nuclear weapons are poor instruments for blackmail, would they not provide a cheap and decisive offensive force when used against a conventionally armed enemy? Some people once thought that South Korea, and earlier, the Shah's Iran, wanted nuclear weapons for offensive use. Yet one can neither say why South Korea would have used nuclear weapons against fellow Koreans while trying to reunite them nor how it could have used nuclear weapons against the North, knowing that China and the Soviet Union might have retaliated. And what goals might a conventionally strong Iran have entertained that would have tempted it to risk using nuclear weapons? A country that launches a strike has to fear a punishing blow from someone. Far from lowering the expected cost of aggression, a nuclear offense even against a nonnuclear state raises the possible costs of aggression to incalculable heights because the aggressor cannot be sure of the reaction of other states.

Nuclear weapons do not make nuclear war likely, as history has shown. The point made when discussing the internal use of nuclear weapons bears repeating. No one can say that nuclear weapons will never be used. Their use is always possible. In asking what the spread of nuclear weapons will do to the world, we are asking about the effects to be expected if a larger number of relatively weak states get nuclear weapons. If such states use nuclear weapons, the world will not end. The use of nuclear weapons by lesser powers would hardly trigger them elsewhere.

DETERRENCE BY SMALL NUCLEAR FORCES

How hard is it for minor nuclear powers to build deterrent forces? In this section, I answer the question.

The Problems of Preventive and Preemptive Strikes[16]

The first danger posed by the spread of nuclear weapons would seem to be that each new nuclear state may tempt an older one to strike to destroy an embryonic nuclear capability before it can become militarily effective. As more countries acquire nuclear weapons, and as more countries gain nuclear competence through power projects, the difficulties and dangers of making preventive strikes increase. Because of America's nuclear arsenal, the Soviet Union could hardly have destroyed the budding forces of Britain and France; but the United States could have struck the Soviet Union's early nuclear facilities, and the United States or the Soviet Union could have struck China's. Long before Israel struck Iraq's reactor, preventive strikes were treated as more than abstract possibilities. When Francis P. Matthews was President Harry S. Truman's secretary of the Navy, he made a speech that seemed to favor our waging a preventive war. The United States, he urged, should be willing to pay "even the price of instituting a war to compel cooperation for peace."[17] Moreover, preventive strikes against nuclear installations can be made by nonnuclear states and have sometimes been threatened. Thus President Nasser warned Israel in 1960 that Egypt would attack if it were sure that Israel was building a bomb. "It is inevitable," he said, "that we should attack the base of aggression even if we have to mobilize four million to destroy it."[18]

The uneven development of the forces of potential and of new nuclear states creates occasions that permit strikes and may invite them. Two stages of nuclear development should be distinguished. First, a country may be in an early stage of nuclear development and be obviously unable to make nuclear weapons. Second, a country may be in an advanced stage of nuclear development, and whether or not it has some nuclear weapons may not be surely known. All of the present nuclear countries went through both stages, yet until Israel struck Iraq's nuclear facility in June of 1981, no one had launched a preventive strike.

A number of causes combined may account for the reluctance of states to strike in order to prevent adversaries from developing nuclear forces. A preventive strike is most promising during the first stage of nuclear development. A state could strike without fearing that the country it attacked would be able to return a nuclear blow. But would one country strike so hard as to destroy another country's potential for future nuclear development? If it did not, the country struck could resume its nuclear career. If the blow struck is less than devastating, one must be prepared either to repeat it or to occupy and control the country. To do either would be forbiddingly difficult.

In striking Iraq, Israel showed that a preventive strike can be made, something that was not in doubt. Israel's act and its consequences, however, made clear that the likelihood of useful accomplishment is low. Israel's action increased the determination of Arabs to produce nuclear weapons. Israel's strike, far from foreclosing

Iraq's nuclear career, gained Iraq support from some other Arab states to pursue it. Despite Prime Minister Menachem Begin's vow to strike as often as need be, the risks in doing so would have risen with each occasion.

A preemptive strike launched against a country that may have a small number of warheads is even less promising than a preventive strike during the first stage. If the country attacked has even a rudimentary nuclear capability, one's own severe punishment becomes possible. Nuclear forces are seldom delicate because no state wants delicate forces, and nuclear forces can easily be made sturdy. Nuclear warheads can be fairly small and light, and they are easy to hide and to move. Even the Model-T bombs dropped on Hiroshima and Nagasaki were small enough to fit into a World War II bomber. Early in the nuclear age, people worried about atomic bombs being concealed in packing boxes and placed in the holds of ships to be exploded when a signal was given. Now, more than ever, people worry about terrorists stealing nuclear warheads because various states have so many of them. Everybody seems to believe that terrorists are capable of hiding bombs.[19] Why should states be unable to do what terrorist gangs are thought to be capable of?

It was sometimes claimed that a small number of bombs in the hands of minor powers would create greater dangers than additional thousands in the hands of the United States or the Soviet Union. Such statements assume that preemption of a small force is easy. Acting on that assumption, someone may be tempted to strike; fearing this, the state with the small number of weapons may be tempted to use the few weapons it has rather than risk losing them. Such reasoning would confirm the thought that small nuclear forces create extreme dangers. But since protecting small forces by hiding and moving them is quite easy, the dangers evaporate.

Requirements of Deterrence

To be effective, deterrent forces, whether big or small ones, must meet these requirements. First, at least a part of a state's nuclear forces must appear to be able to survive an attack and launch one of its own. Second, survival of forces must not require early firing in response to what may be false alarms. Third, command and control must be reliably maintained; weapons must not be susceptible to accidental or unauthorized use.[20]

The first two requirements are closely linked both to each other and to measures needed to ensure that deterrent forces cannot be preempted. If states can deploy their forces in ways that preclude preemption—and we have seen that they can—then their forces need not be rigged for hair-trigger response. States can retaliate at their leisure.

This question then arises: May dispersing forces for the sake of their survival make command and control hard to maintain? Americans think so because we think in terms of large nuclear arsenals. Small nuclear powers neither have them nor need them. Lesser nuclear states may deploy, say, ten real weapons and ten dummies, while permitting other countries to infer that numbers are larger. An adversary need only believe that some warheads may survive its attack and be visited on it. That belief is not hard to create without making command and control unreliable. All nuclear countries live through a time when their forces are crudely designed. All countries have so far been able to control them. Relations between the United States and the Soviet Union, and later among the United States, the Soviet Union, and China, were at their bitterest just when their nuclear forces were in early stages of development and were unbalanced, crude, and presumably hard to control. Why should we expect new nuclear states to experience greater difficulties than the ones old nuclear states were able to cope with? Although some of the new nuclear states may be economically and technically backward, they will either have expert and highly trained scientists and engineers or they will not be able to produce nuclear weapons. Even if they buy or steal the weapons, they will have to hire technicians to maintain and control them. We do not have to wonder whether they will take good care of their weapons. They have every incentive to do so. They will not want to risk retaliation because one or more of their warheads accidentally struck another country.

Hiding nuclear weapons and keeping them under control are tasks for which the ingenuity of numerous states is adequate. Means of delivery are neither difficult to devise nor hard to procure. Bombs can be driven in by trucks from neighboring countries. Ports can be torpedoed by small boats lying offshore. A thriving arms trade in ever more sophisticated military equipment provides ready access to what may be wanted, including planes and missiles suited to the delivery of nuclear warheads.

Lesser nuclear states can pursue deterrent strategies effectively. Deterrence requires the ability to inflict unacceptable damage on another country. ``Unacceptable damage'' to the Soviet Union was variously defined by Robert McNamara as requiring the ability to destroy a fifth to a fourth of its population and a half to two-thirds of its industrial capacity. American estimates of what is required for deterrence were absurdly high. To deter, a country need not appear to be able to destroy a fourth or a half of another country, although in some cases that might be easily done. Would Libya try to destroy Israel's nuclear weapons at the risk of two bombs surviving to fall on Tripoli and Bengazi? And what would be left of Israel if Tel Aviv and Haifa were destroyed?

The weak can deter one another. But can the weak deter the strong? Raising the question of China's ability to deter the Soviet Union in the old days highlights the issue. The population and industry of most states concentrate in a relatively small number of centers. This was true of the Soviet Union. A major attack on the top ten cities of the Soviet Union would have mashed 25 percent of its industrial capacity and 25 percent of its urban population. Geoffrey Kemp in 1974 concluded that China could probably have struck on that scale.[21] And I emphasize again, China needed only to *appear* to be able to do that. A low probability of carrying a highly destructive attack home is sufficient for deterrence. A force of an imprecisely specifiable minimum capacity is nevertheless needed.

In a 1979 study, Justin Galen (pseud.) wondered whether the Chinese had a force capable of deterring the Soviet Union. He estimated that China had sixty to eighty medium-range and sixty to eighty intermediate-range missiles of doubtful reliability and accuracy and eighty obsolete bombers. He rightly pointed out that the missiles might miss their targets even if fired at cities and that the bombers might not get through the Soviet Union's defenses. Moreover, the Soviet Union might have been able to preempt an attack, having almost certainly "located virtually every Chinese missile, aircraft, weapons storage area and production facility."[22] But surely Soviet leaders put these things the other way around. To locate virtually all missiles and aircraft is not good enough. Despite inaccuracies a few Chinese missiles might have hit Russian cities, and some bombers might have got through. Not much is required to deter. What political-military objective is worth risking Vladivostok, Novosibirsk, and Tomsk, with no way of being sure that Moscow would not go as well?

The Credibility of Small Deterrent Forces

The credibility of weaker countries' deterrent threats has two faces. The first is physical. Will such countries be able to construct and protect a deliverable force? We have found that they can quite readily do so. The second is psychological. Will deterrent threats that are physically feasible be psychologically plausible? Will an adversary believe that the retaliation that is threatened will be carried out?

Deterrent threats backed by second-strike nuclear forces raise the possible costs of an attack to such heights that war becomes unlikely. But deterrent threats may not be credible. In a world where two or more countries can make them, the prospect of *mutual* devastation may make it difficult, or irrational, to execute threats should the occasion for doing so arise. Would it not be senseless to risk suffering further destruction once a deterrent force had failed to deter? Believing that it would be, an adversary may attack counting on the attacked country's unwillingness to risk initiating a devastating exchange by its own retaliation. Why retaliate once a threat to do so has failed? If one's policy is to rely on forces designed to deter, then an attack that is nevertheless made shows that one's reliance was misplaced. The course of wisdom may be to pose a new question: What is the best policy once deterrence has failed? One gains nothing by destroying an enemy's cities. Instead, in retaliating, one may prompt the enemy to unleash more warheads. A ruthless aggressor may strike believing that the leaders of the attacked country are capable of following such a "rational" line of thought. To carry the threat out may be "irrational." This old worry achieved new prominence as the strategic capabilities of the Soviet Union approached those of the United States in the middle 1970s. The Soviet Union, some feared, might believe that the United States would be self-deterred.[23]

Much of the literature on deterrence emphasizes the problem of achieving the credibility on which deterrence depends and the danger of relying on a deterrent of uncertain credibility. One earlier solution of the problem was found in Thomas Schelling's notion of "the threat that leaves something to chance."[24] No state can know for sure that another state will refrain from retaliating even when retaliation would be irrational. No state can bet heavily on another state's common sense. Bernard Brodie put the thought more directly, while avoiding the slippery notion of rationality. Rather than ask what it may be rational or irrational for governments to do, the question he repeatedly asked was this: How do governments behave in the presence of awesome dangers? His answer was, very carefully.

To ask why a country should carry out its deterrent threat if deterrence fails is to ask the wrong question. The question suggests that an aggressor may attack believing that the attacked country may not retaliate. This invokes the conventional logic that analysts find so hard to forsake. In a conventional world, a country can sensibly attack if it believes that success is possible. In a nuclear world, a would-be attacker is deterred if it believes that the attacked *may* retaliate. Uncertainty of response, not certainty, is required for deterrence because, if retaliation occurs, one risks losing so much. In a nuclear world, we should look less at the retaliator's conceivable inhibitions and more at the challenger's obvious risks.

One may nevertheless wonder whether retaliatory threats remain credible if the strategic forces of the attacker are superior to those of the attacked. Will an unsuccessful defender in a conventional war have the courage to unleash its deterrent force, using nuclear weapons first against a country having superior strategic forces? Once more this asks the wrong question. The would-be attacker will ask itself, not whose forces are numerically superior, but whether a grossly provoca-tive act might bring nuclear warheads down on itself. When vital interests are at stake, all of the parties involved are strongly constrained to be moderate because one's immoderate behavior makes the nuclear threats of others credible.

With deterrent forces, the question is not whether one country has more than another but whether it has the capability of inflicting "unacceptable damage" on another, with "unacceptable" sensibly defined. Given second-strike capabilities, it is not the balance of forces but the possibility that they may be used that counts. The balance or imbalance of strategic forces affects neither the calculation of danger nor the question of whose will is the stronger. Second-strike forces have to be seen in absolute terms.

Emphasizing the importance of the "balance of resolve," to use Glenn Snyder's apt phrase, raises questions about what a deterrent force covers and what it does not.[25] In answering these questions, we can learn something from the experience of the Cold War. The United States and the Soviet Union limited their provocative acts, the more carefully so when major values for one side or the other were at issue. This can be seen both in what they did and in what they did not do. Whatever support the Soviet Union gave to North Korea's attack on the South in June of 1950 was given after Secretary of State Acheson, the Joint Chiefs of Staff, General MacArthur, the chairman of the Senate Foreign Relations Committee, and others explicitly excluded both South Korea and Taiwan from America's defense perimeter. The United States, to take another example, could fight for years on a large scale in Southeast Asia because neither success nor failure mattered much internationally. Victory would not have made the world one of American hegemony. Defeat would not have made the world one of Soviet hegemony. No vital interest of either superpower was at stake, as both Kissinger and Brezhnev made clear at the time.[26] One can fight without fearing escalation only where little is at stake. That is where the deterrent does not deter.

Actions at the periphery can safely be bolder than actions at the center. In contrast, where much is at stake for one side, the other side moves with care. Trying to win where winning would bring the central balance into question threatens escalation and becomes too risky to contemplate. The United States was circumspect when East European crises loomed in the mid-1950s. Thus Secretary of State Dulles assured the Soviet Union, when Hungarians rebelled in October of 1956, that we would not interfere with Soviet efforts to suppress them. And the Soviet Union's moves in the center of Europe were carefully controlled. Its probes in Berlin were tentative, reversible, and ineffective. Strikingly, the long border between Eastern and Western Europe—drawn where borders earlier proved unstable—was free even of skirmishes through all of the years after the Second World War.

Contemplating American and Soviet postwar behavior, and interpreting it in terms of nuclear logic, suggests that deterrence extends to vital interests beyond the homeland more easily than most have thought. The United States cared more about Western Europe than the Soviet Union did. The Soviet Union cared more about Eastern Europe than the United States did. Communicating the weight of one side's concern as compared to the other side's was easily enough done when the matters at hand affected the United States and the Soviet Union directly. For this reason, West European anxiety about the coverage it got from our strategic forces, while understandable, was grossly exaggerated. The United States might have retaliated if the Soviet Union had made a major military move against a NATO country, and that alone was enough to deter the Soviet Union.

The Problem of Extended Deterrence

How far from the homeland does deterrence extend? One answers that question by defining the conditions that must obtain if deterrent threats are to be credited.

First, the would-be attacker must be made to see that the deterrer considers the interests at stake to be vital. One cannot assume that countries will instantly agree on the question of whose interests are vital. Nuclear weapons, however, strongly incline them to grope for *de facto* agreement on the answer rather than to fight over it.

Second, political stability must prevail in the area that the deterrent is intended to cover. If the threat to a regime is in good part from internal factions, then an outside power may risk supporting one of them even in the face of deterrent threats. The credibility of a deterrent force requires both that interests be seen to be vital and that it is an attack from outside that threatens them. Given these conditions, the would-be attacker provides both the reason to retaliate and the target for retaliation.

The problem of stretching a deterrent, which agitated the western alliance, is not a problem for lesser nuclear states. Their problem is not to protect others but to protect themselves. Many fear that lesser nuclear states will be the first ones to break the nuclear taboo and that they will use their weapons irresponsibly. I expect the opposite. Weak states easily establish their credibility. They are not trying to stretch their deterrent forces to cover others, and their vulnerability to conventional attack lends credence to their nuclear threats. Because in a conventional war they can lose so much so fast, it is easy to believe that they will unleash a deterrent force even at the risk of receiving a nuclear blow in return. With deterrent forces, the party that is absolutely threatened prevails.[27] Use of nuclear weapons by lesser states, or by any state, will come only if survival is at stake. This should be called not irresponsible but responsible use.

An opponent who attacks what is unambiguously mine risks suffering great distress if I have second-strike forces. This statement has important implications for both the deterrer and the deterred. Where territorial claims are shadowy and disputed, deterrent writs do not run. As Steven J. Rosen has said, "It is difficult to imagine Israel committing national suicide to hold on to Abu Rudeis or Hebron or Mount Hermon."[28] Establishing the credibility of a deterrent force requires moderation of territorial claims on the part of the would-be deterrer. For modest states, weapons whose very existence works strongly against their use are just what is wanted.

In a nuclear world, conservative would-be attackers will be prudent, but will would-be attackers be conservative? A new Hitler is not unimaginable. Would the presence of nuclear weapons have moderated Hitler's behavior? Hitler did not start World War II in order to destroy the Third Reich. Indeed, he was dismayed by British and French declarations of war on Poland's behalf. After all, the western democracies had not come to the aid of a geographically defensible and militarily strong Czechoslovakia. Why then should they have declared war on behalf of an indefensible Poland and against a Germany made stronger by the incorporation of Czechoslovakia's armor? From the occupation of the Rhineland in 1936 to the invasion of Poland in 1939, Hitler's calculations were realistically made. In those years, Hitler would have been deterred from acting in ways that immediately threatened massive death and widespread destruction in Germany. And, even if Hitler had not been deterred, would his generals have obeyed his commands? In a nuclear world, to act in blatantly offensive ways is madness. Under the circumstances, how many generals would obey the commands of a madman? One man alone does not make war.

To believe that nuclear deterrence would have worked against Germany in 1939 is easy. It is also easy to believe that in 1945, given the ability to do so, Hitler and some few around him would have fired nuclear warheads at the United States, Great Britain, and the Soviet Union as their armies advanced, whatever the consequences for Germany. Two considerations work against this possibility: the first applies in any world; the second in a nuclear world. First, when defeat is seen to be inevitable, a ruler's authority may vanish. Early in 1945, Hitler apparently ordered the initiation of gas warfare, but his generals did not respond.[29] Second, no country will press another to the point of decisive defeat. In the desperation of defeat, desperate measures may be taken, and the last thing anyone wants to do is to make a nuclear nation desperate. The unconditional surrender of a nuclear nation cannot be demanded. Nuclear weapons affect the deterrer as well as the deterred.

ARMS RACES AMONG NEW NUCLEAR STATES

One may believe that old American and Soviet military doctrines set the pattern that new nuclear states will follow. One may also believe that they will suffer the fate of the United States and the former Soviet Union, that they will compete in building larger and larger nuclear arsenals while continuing to accumulate conventional weapons. These are doubtful beliefs. One can infer the future from the past only insofar as future situations may be like past ones for the actors involved. For three main reasons, new nuclear states are likely to decrease, rather than to increase, their military spending.

First, nuclear weapons alter the dynamics of arms races. In a competition of two or more parties, it may be hard to say who is pushing and who is being pushed, who is leading and who is following. If one party seeks to increase its capabilities, it may seem that others must too. The dynamic may be built into the competition and may unfold despite a mutual wish to resist it. But need this be the case in a strategic competition among nuclear countries? It need not be if the conditions of competition make deterrent logic dominant. Deterrent logic domi-

nates if the conditions of competition make it nearly impossible for any of the competing parties to achieve a
first-strike capability. Early in the nuclear age, the implications of deterrent strategy were clearly seen. "When
dealing with the absolute weapon," as William T. R. Fox
put it, "arguments based on relative advantage lose their
point."[30] The United States has sometimes designed its
forces according to that logic. Donald A. Quarles, when
he was President Eisenhower's secretary of the Air
Force, argued that "sufficiency of air power" is determined by "the force required to accomplish the mission
assigned." Avoidance of total war then does not depend
on the "*relative* strength of the two opposed forces." Instead, it depends on the "*absolute* power in the hands of
each, and in the substantial invulnerability of this power
to interdiction."[31] To repeat: If no state can launch a disarming attack with high confidence, force comparisons
are irrelevant. Strategic arms races are then pointless.
Deterrent strategies offer this great advantage: Within
wide ranges neither side need respond to increases in
the other side's military capabilities.

Those who foresee nuclear arms racing among new
nuclear states fail to make the distinction between war-
fighting and war-deterring capabilities. War-fighting
forces, because they threaten the forces of others, have to
be compared. Superior forces may bring victory to one
country; inferior forces may bring defeat to another.
Force requirements vary with strategies and not just with
the characteristics of weapons. With war-fighting strategies, arms races become hard to avoid. Forces designed
for deterrence need not be compared. As Harold Brown
said when he was secretary of Defense, purely deterrent
forces "can be relatively modest, and their size can perhaps be made substantially, though not completely, insensitive to changes in the posture of an opponent."[32]
With deterrent strategies, arms races make sense only if
a first-strike capability is within reach. Because thwarting

a first strike is easy, deterrent forces are quite cheap to build and maintain.

Second, deterrent balances are inherently stable. This is another reason for new nuclear states to decrease, rather than increase, their military spending. As Secretary Brown saw, within wide limits one state can be insensitive to changes in another state's forces. French leaders thought this way. France, as President Valéry Giscard d'Estaing said, "fixes its security at the level required to maintain, regardless of the way the strategic situation develops in the world, the credibility—in other words, the effectiveness—of its deterrent force."[33] With deterrent forces securely established, no military requirement presses one side to try to surpass the other. Human error and folly may lead some parties involved in deterrent balances to spend more on armaments than is needed, but other parties need not increase their armaments in response, because such excess spending does not threaten them. The logic of deterrence eliminates incentives for strategic-arms racing. This should be easier for lesser nuclear states to understand than it was for the United States and the Soviet Union. Because most of them are economically hard-pressed, they will not want to have more than enough.

Allowing for their particular situations, the policies of nuclear states confirm these statements. Britain and France are relatively rich countries, and they have tended to overspend. Their strategic forces were nevertheless modest enough when one considers that they thought that to deter the Soviet Union would be more difficult than to deter states with capabilities comparable to their own. China of course faced the same task. These three countries however, have shown no inclination to engage in nuclear arms races. India was content to have a nuclear military capability that may or may not have produced warheads, and Israel long maintained her ambiguous status. New nuclear states are likely to conform to these patterns and aim for a modest sufficiency rather than vie with one another for a meaningless superiority.

Third, because strategic nuclear arms races among lesser powers are unlikely, the interesting question is not whether they will be run but whether countries having strategic nuclear weapons can avoid running conventional races. No more than the United States will new nuclear states want to rely on executing the deterrent threat that risks all. Will not their vulnerability to conventional attack induce them at least to maintain their conventional forces?

American policy since the early 1960s again teaches lessons that mislead. From President John F. Kennedy and Secretary Robert S. McNamara onward, the United States followed a policy of flexible response, emphasizing the importance of having a continuum of forces that would enable the United States to fight at any level from irregular to strategic nuclear warfare. A policy that decreases reliance on deterrence by placing more emphasis on conventional forces would seem to increase the chances that wars will be fought. Americans wanted to avoid nuclear war in Europe. Europeans wanted to avoid any war in Europe. Flexible response weakened Europeans' confidence in America's deterrent forces. Their worries were well expressed by a senior British general: "McNamara is practically telling the Soviets that the worst they need expect from an attack on West Germany is a conventional counterattack."[34] Why risk one's own destruction if one is able to fight on the ground and forego the use of strategic weapons? The policy of flexible response seemed to lessen reliance on deterrence and to increase the chances of fighting a war, although not nearly as much as the unnamed British general thought.

Large conventional forces neither add to nor subtract from the credibility of second-strike nuclear forces. Smaller nuclear states are likely to understand this more easily than the United States and the Soviet Union did, if only because few of them can afford to combine deterrent with large war-fighting forces.

Israel's military policy seems to fly in the face of deterrent logic. Its military budget has at times exceeded 20 percent of its GDP.[35] In fact Israel's policy bears deterrent logic out. So long as Israel continues to hold the Golan Heights and parts of the West Bank, it has to be prepared to fight for them. Since they by no means belong unambiguously to Israel, deterrent threats do not cover them. Because of America's large subsidies, economic constraints have not driven Israel to the territorial settlement that would shrink its borders sufficiently to make a deterrent policy credible. Global and regional forces, however, now do so. To compete internationally, Israel has to reduce its military expenditures. If a state's borders encompass only its vital interests, their protection does not require spending large sums on conventional forces.

The success of a deterrent strategy depends neither on the conventional capabilities of states nor on the extent of territory they hold. States can safely shrink their borders because defense in depth becomes irrelevant. The point can be put the other way around: With deterrent forces, arms races in their ultimate form—the fighting of offensive wars designed to increase national security—become pointless.

THE FREQUENCY AND INTENSITY OF WAR

The presence of nuclear weapons makes war less likely. One may nevertheless oppose the spread of nuclear weapons on the ground that they would make war, however unlikely, unbearably intense should it occur. Nuclear weapons have not been fired in anger in a world in which more than one country has them. We have enjoyed half a century of nuclear peace, but we can never have a guarantee. We may be grateful for decades of nuclear peace and for the discouragement of conventional war among those who have nuclear weapons. Yet the fear is widespread that if they ever go off, we may all be dead. People as varied as the scholar Richard Smoke, the arms controller Paul Warnke, and the former defense secretary Harold Brown have all believed that if any nuclear weapons go off, many will. Although this seems the least likely of all the unlikely possibilities, it is not impossible. What makes it so unlikely is that, if a few warheads are fired, all of the countries involved will want to get out of the mess they are in.

McNamara asked himself what fractions of the Soviet Union's population and industry the United States should be able to destroy to deter it. This was the wrong question. States are not deterred because they expect to suffer a certain amount of damage but because they cannot know how much damage they will suffer. Near the dawn of the nuclear age, Bernard Brodie put the matter simply, "The prediction is more important than the fact."[36] The prediction, that is, that attacking the vital interests of a country having nuclear weapons may bring the attacker untold losses. As Patrick Morgan later put it, "To attempt to compute the cost of a nuclear war is to miss the point."[37]

States are deterred by the prospect of suffering severe damage and by their inability to do much to limit it. Deterrence works because nuclear weapons enable one state to punish another state severely without first defeating it. "Victory," in Thomas Schelling's words, "is no longer a prerequisite for hurting the enemy."[38] Countries armed only with conventional weapons can hope that their military forces will be able to limit the damage an attacker can do. Among countries armed with strategic nuclear forces, the hope of avoiding heavy damage depends mainly on the attacker's restraint and little on one's own efforts. Those who compared expected deaths through strategic exchanges of nuclear warheads with casualties suffered by the Soviet Union in World War II overlooked the fundamental difference between conventional and nuclear worlds.[39]

Deterrence rests on what countries *can* do to each other with strategic nuclear weapons. From this statement, one easily leaps to the wrong conclusion: that deterrent strategies, if they have to be carried through, will produce a catastrophe. That countries are able to annihilate each other means neither that deterrence depends on their threatening to do so nor that they will do so if deterrence fails. Because countries heavily armed with strategic nuclear weapons can carry war to its ultimate intensity, the control of force becomes the primary objective. If deterrence fails, leaders will have the strongest incentives to keep force under control and limit damage rather than launching genocidal attacks. If the Soviet Union had attacked Western Europe, NATO's objectives would have been to halt the attack and end the war. The United States had the ability to place thousands of warheads precisely on targets in the Soviet Union. Surely we would have struck military targets before striking industrial targets and industrial targets before striking cities. The intent to hit military targets first was sometimes confused with a war-fighting strategy, but it was not one. It would not have significantly reduced the Soviet Union's ability to hurt us. Whatever American military leaders thought, our strategy rested on the threat to punish. The threat, if it failed to deter, would have been followed not by spasms of violence but by punishment administered in ways that conveyed threats of more to come.

A war between the United States and the Soviet Union that got out of control would have been catastrophic. If they had set out to destroy each other, they would have greatly reduced the world's store of developed resources while killing millions outside of their own borders through fallout. Even while destroying themselves, states with few weapons would do less damage to others. As ever, the biggest international dangers come from the strongest states. Fearing the world's destruction, one may prefer a world of conventional great powers having a higher probability of fighting less-destructive wars to a world of nuclear great powers having a lower probability of fighting more-destructive wars. But that choice effectively disappeared with the production of atomic bombs by the United States during World War II.

Does the spread of nuclear weapons threaten to make wars more intense at regional levels, where wars of high intensity have been possible for many years? If weaker countries are unable to defend at lesser levels of violence, might they destroy themselves through resorting to nuclear weapons? Lesser nuclear states live in fear of this possibility. But this is not different from the fear under which the United States and the Soviet Union lived for years. Small nuclear states may experience a keen sense of desperation because of vulnerability to conventional as well as to nuclear attack, but, again, in desperate situations what all parties become most desperate to avoid is the use of strategic nuclear weapons. Still, however improbable the event, lesser states may one day fire some of their weapons. Are minor nuclear states more or less likely to do so than major ones? The answer to this question is vitally important because the existence of some states would be at stake even if the damage done were regionally confined.

For a number of reasons, deterrent strategies promise less damage than war-fighting strategies. First, deterrent strategies induce caution all around and thus reduce the incidence of war. Second, wars fought in the face of strategic nuclear weapons must be carefully limited because a country having them may retaliate if its vital interests are threatened. Third, prospective punishment need only be proportionate to an adversary's expected gains in war after those gains are discounted for the many uncertainties of war. Fourth, should deterrence fail, a few judiciously delivered warheads are likely to produce sobriety in the leaders of all of the countries involved and thus bring rapid deescalation. Finally, warfighting strategies offer no clear place to stop short of victory for some and defeat for others. Deterrent strategies do, and that place is where one country threatens another's vital interests. Deterrent strategies lower the probability that wars will begin. If wars start nevertheless, deterrent strategies lower the probability that they will be carried very far.

Nuclear weapons lessen the intensity as well as the frequency of war among their possessors. For fear of escalation, nuclear states do not want to fight long and hard over important interests—indeed, they do not want to fight at all. Minor nuclear states have even better reasons than major ones to accommodate one another and to avoid fighting. Worries about the intensity of war among nuclear states have to be viewed in this context and against a world in which conventional weapons have become ever costlier and more destructive.

THE RECENT SPREAD OF NUCLEAR WEAPONS[40]

As I write this paper in July of 1994, the American government, the press, and much of the public are agitated by the possibility that North Korea has, or will soon have, nuclear weapons.

The United States opposes North Korea's presumed quest for nuclear military capability, yet in the past half-century, no country has been able to prevent other countries from going nuclear if they were determined to do so. Sometimes we have helped them, as with Britain and France, sometimes we have looked the other way, as with Israel, and sometimes we have tried and failed to persuade countries to forego the capability.

In all previous cases, the United States was constrained by interests beyond our concern for slowing the
spread of nuclear weapons. During the Cold War we did
not want to drive India more deeply into the arms of the
Soviet Union, and we valued the cooperation of Pakistan. Even though China, South Korea, and Japan have
opposed sanctions against North Korea, America sees itself as being less constrained this time. We have maneu-
vered and threatened to get North Korea to observe the
nuclear Non-Proliferation Treaty's inspection provisions.
But even if it does, what will we learn?

David T. French, spokeman for the CIA, described
North Korea as being "impossible to penetrate."[41] Andrew Hanami thinks that North Korea may have dug
11,000 tunnels, good places for hiding warheads.[42]
Guesses about the number of nuclear sites in North Korea vary. We know that North Korea will never allow inspectors to roam the land freely, and even if they could,
they would never be able to say that they had found all
of the places where bombs may be hidden. Any country
that wants to build warheads, and not be caught doing
it, will disguise its efforts and hide its bombs. After all,
even with numerous United Nations inspectors romping
around Iraq, we still do not know for sure what facilities
and weapons it does and does not have.

Like earlier nuclear states, North Korea wants the
military capability because it feels weak, isolated, and
threatened. The ratio of South Korea's to North Korea's
GDP in 1992 was 14:1; of their populations, 2:1; of their
defense budgets, 2:1.[43] North Korea does have twice as
large an active army and twice as many tanks, but their
quality is low, spare parts and fuel scarce, training limited, and communications and logistics dated. In addition, South Korea has the backing of the United States
and the presence of American troops.

Despite North Korea's weakness, some people,
Americans especially, worry that the North might invade

the South, even using nuclear weapons in doing so. How concerned should we be? No one has figured out how to use nuclear weapons except for deterrence. Is a small and weak state likely to be the first to do so? Countries that use nuclear weapons have to fear retalition. Why would the North now invade the South? It did in 1950, but only after prominent American congressmen, military leaders, and other officials said that we would not fight in Korea. Any war on the peninsula would put North Korea at severe risk. Perhaps because South Koreans appreciate this fact more keenly than Americans do, relatively few of them seem to believe that North Korea will invade.

Kim Il Sung threatened war, but anyone who thinks that when a dictator threatens war we should believe him is lost wandering around somewhere in a bygone conventional world.[44] Kim Il Sung was sometimes compared with Hitler and Stalin.[45] Despite similarities, it is foolish to forget that North Korea's capabilities in no way compare with the Germany of Hitler or the Soviet Union of Stalin. Nuclear weapons make states more cautious, as the history of the nuclear age shows. "Rogue states," as the Soviet Union and China were once thought to be, have followed the pattern. The weaker and the more endangered a state is, the less likely it is to engage in reckless behavior. North Korea's external behavior has sometimes been ugly, but certainly not reckless. Its regime has shown no inclination to risk suicide. This is one good reason why surrounding states counsel patience.

Senator John McCain, a former naval officer, nevertheless believes that North Korea would be able to attack without fear of failure because a South Korean and American counterattack would have to stop at the present border for fear of North Korean nuclear retaliation.[46] Our vast nuclear forces would not deter an attack on the South, yet the dinky force that the North may have would deter us! A land-war game played by the American military in 1994 showed another side of American military thinking. The game pitted the United States against a Third World country similar to North Korea. Losing conventionally, it struck our forces with nuclear weapons. For unmentioned reasons, our superior military forces had no deterrent effect. Results were said to be devastating. With such possibilities in mind, Air Force General George Lee Butler and his fellow planners called for a new strategy of deterrence, with "generic targeting" so we will be able to strike wherever "terorist states or rogue leaders . . . threaten to use their own nuclear, chemical or biological weapons." The strategy will supposedly deter states or terrorists from brandishing or using their weapons. Yet General Butler himself believes, as I do, that Saddam Hussein was deterred from using chemicals and biologicals in the Gulf War.[47]

During the 1993 American–South Korean "Team Spirit" military exercises, North Korea denied access to International Atomic Energy Agency inspectors and threatened to withdraw from the nuclear Non-Proliferation Treaty. The North's reaction suggests, as one would expect, that the more vulnerable North Korea feels, the more strenuously it will pursue a nuclear program. The pattern has been universal ever since the United States led the way into the nuclear age. Noticing this, we should be careful about conveying military threats to weak states.

One worry remains: A nuclear North Korea would put pressure on South Korea and Japan to develop comparable weapons. Their doing so would hardly be surprising. Nuclear states have tended to come in hostile pairs. American capability led to the Soviet Union's, the Soviet Union's to China's, China's to India's, India's to Pakistan's, and Israel's spurred Iraq's efforts to acquire bombs of its own. Countries are vulnerable to capabilities that they lack and others have. Sooner or later, usually sooner, they try to gain comparable capabilities or seek the protection of states that have them. Do we think we can change age-old patterns of international behavior? A nuclear North Korea is but one reason for other countries in the region to go nuclear, especially when confidence in America's extended deterrent wanes as the bipolar world disappears.

CIA Director James Woolsey has said that he "can think of no example where the introduction of nuclear weapons into a region has enhanced that region's security or benefitted the security interests of the United States."[48] But surely nuclear weapons helped to maintain stability during the Cold War and to preserve peace throughout the instability that came in its wake. Except for interventions by major powers in conflicts that for them were minor, peace has become the privilege of states having nuclear weapons, while wars have been fought mainly by those who lack them. Weak states cannot help noticing this. That is why states feeling threatened want to have their own nuclear weapons and why states that have them find it so hard to halt their spread.

Pakistan is another recent worry. The worry runs to form. When the weak fear the strong, the weaker party does what it can to maintain its security. When asked why nuclear weapons are so popular in Pakistan, Prime Minister Benazir Bhutto answered, "It's our history. A history of three wars with a larger neighbor. India is five times larger than we are. Their military strength is five times larger. In 1971, our country was disintegrated. So the security issue for Pakistan is an issue of survival."[49] From the other side, Shankar Bajpai, former Indian ambassador to Pakistan, China, and the United States, has said that "Pakistan's quest for a nuclear capability stems from its fear of its larger neighbor, removing that fear should open up immense possibilities"—possibilities for a less worried and more relaxed life.[50]

CONCLUSION

The conclusion is in two parts. The first part applies the above analysis to the present. The second part uses it to peer into the future.

What Follows from My Analysis?

I have argued that the gradual spread of nuclear weapons is better than either no spread or rapid spread. We do not face happy choices. We may prefer that countries have conventional weapons only, do not run arms races, and do not fight. Yet the alternative to nuclear weapons may be ruinous arms races for some countries with a high risk of their becoming engaged in devastating conventional wars.

Countries have to take care of their own security. If countries feel insecure and believe that nuclear weapons would make them more secure, America's policy of opposing the spread of nuclear weapons will not prevail. Any slight chance of bringing the spread of nuclear weapons to a halt exists only if the United States strenuously tries to achieve that end. To do so carries costs measured in terms of other interests. The strongest way for the United States to persuade other countries to forego nuclear weapons is to guarantee their security. How many states' security do we want to guarantee? Wisely, we are reluctant to make promises, but then we should not expect to decide how other countries provide for their security.

Some have feared that weakening opposition to the spread of nuclear weapons will lead numerous states to obtain them because it may seem that "everyone is doing it."[51] Why should we think that if we relax, numerous states will begin to make nuclear weapons? Both the United States and the Soviet Union were relaxed in the past, and those effects did not follow. The Soviet Union initially supported China's nuclear program. The United

States helped both Britain and France to produce nuclear weapons. By 1968 the CIA had informed President Johnson of the existence of Israeli nuclear weapons, and in July of 1970, Richard Helms, director of the CIA, gave this information to the Senate Foreign Relations Committee. These and later disclosures were not followed by censure of Israel or by reductions of economic assistance.[52] And in September of 1980, the executive branch, against the will of the House of Representatives but with the approval of the Senate, continued to do nuclear business with India despite its explosion of a nuclear device and despite its unwillingness to sign the nuclear Non-Proliferation Treaty.

Many more countries can make nuclear weapons than do. One can believe that American opposition to nuclear arming stays the deluge only by overlooking the complications of international life. Any state has to examine many conditions before deciding whether or not to develop nuclear weapons. Our opposition is only one factor and is not likely to be the decisive one. Many states feel fairly secure living with their neighbors. Why should they want nuclear weapons? Some countries, feeling threatened, have found security through their own strenuous efforts and through arrangements made with others. South Korea is an outstanding example. Many officials believe that South Korea would lose more in terms of American support if it acquired nuclear weapons than it would gain by having them.[53] Further, on occasion we might slow the spread of nuclear weapons by *not* opposing the nuclear weapons programs of some countries. When we oppose Pakistan's nuclear program, we are saying that we disapprove of countries developing nuclear weapons no matter what their neighbors do.

The gradual spread of nuclear weapons has not opened the nuclear floodgates. Nations attend to their security in ways they think best. The fact that so many more countries can make nuclear weapons than do says more about the hesitation of countries to enter the nuclear military business than about the effectiveness of American nonproliferation policy. We should suit our policy to individual cases, sometimes bringing pressure against a country moving toward nuclear-weapons capability and sometimes quietly acquiescing. No one policy is right in all cases. We should ask what the interests of other countries require before putting pressure on them. Some countries are likely to suffer more in cost and pain if they remain conventional states than if they become nuclear ones. The measured spread of nuclear weapons does not run against our interests and can increase the security of some states at a price they can afford to pay.

What Does the Nuclear Future Hold?

What will a world populated by a larger number of nuclear states look like? I have drawn a picture of such a world that accords with experience throughout the nuclear age. Those who dread a world with more nuclear states do little more than assert that more is worse and claim without substantiation that new nuclear states will be less responsible and less capable of self control than the old ones have been. They feel fears that many felt when they imagined how a nuclear China would behave. Such fears have proved unfounded as nuclear weapons have slowly spread. I have found many reasons for believing that with more nuclear states the world will have a promising future. I have reached this unusual conclusion for four main reasons.

First, international politics is a self-help system, and in such systems the principal parties determine their own fate, the fate of other parties, and the fate of the system. This will continue to be so.

Second, given the massive numbers of American and Russian warheads, and given the impossibility of one side destroying enough of the other side's missiles to make a retaliatory strike bearable, the balance of terror is indestructible. What can lesser states do to disrupt the nuclear equilibrium if even the mighty efforts of the United States and the Soviet Union did not shake it?

Third, nuclear weaponry makes miscalculation difficult because it is hard not to be aware of how much damage a small number of warheads can do. Early in this century Norman Angell argued that war could not occur because it would not pay.[54] But conventional wars have brought political gains to some countries at the expense of others. Among nuclear countries, possible losses in war overwhelm possible gains. In the nuclear age Angell's dictum becomes persuasive. When the active use of force threatens to bring great losses, war becomes less likely. This proposition is widely accepted but insufficiently emphasized. Nuclear weapons reduced the chances of war between the United States and the Soviet Union and between the Soviet Union and China. One must expect them to have similar effects elsewhere. Where nuclear weapons threaten to make the cost of wars immense, who will dare to start them?

Fourth, new nuclear states will feel the constraints that present nuclear states have experienced. New nuclear states will be more concerned for their safety and more mindful of dangers than some of the old ones have been. Until recently, only the great and some of the major powers have had nuclear weapons. While nuclear weapons have spread, conventional weapons have proliferated. Under these circumstances, wars have been fought not at the center but at the periphery of international politics. The likelihood of war decreases as deterrent and defensive capabilities increase. Nuclear weapons make wars hard to start. These statements hold for small as for big nuclear powers. Because they do, the gradual spread of nuclear weapons is more to be welcomed than feared.

Chapter 2

MORE WILL BE WORSE

Scott D. Sagan

Why should we worry about the spread of nuclear weapons? The answer is by no means obvious. After all, we have lived with nuclear deterrence for half a century now. The two superpowers maintained a long peace throughout the Cold War, despite deep political hostilities, numerous crises, and a prolonged arms race. Why should we expect that the experience of future nuclear powers will be any different?

A prominent group of scholars have pointed to the apparent contradiction between a peaceful nuclear past and a fearful nuclear future and argue that the further spread of nuclear weapons may well be a stabilizing factor in international relations. In Chapter 1, Kenneth Waltz presents the strongest and most sustained set of arguments in support of this thesis.[1] It is important to note from the start, however, that Waltz is by no means alone in holding this position, as a number of other political scientists have jumped onto the pro-proliferation bandwagon. For example, Bruce Bueno de Mesquita and William Riker advocate the "selective" spread of nuclear weapons into areas where nonnuclear states face nuclear-

This is a revised version of my "The Perils of Proliferation: Organization Theory, Deterrence Theory, and the Spread of Nuclear Weapons," *International Security* 18, no. 4 (Spring 1994), pp. 66–107.

armed adversaries since "the chance of bilateral conflict becoming nuclear . . . decreases to zero when all nations are nuclear armed."[2] John Mearsheimer also believes that "nuclear weapons are a superb deterrent" and argues that the world would be a safer place if Germany, Ukraine, and Japan became nuclear powers in the post– Cold War era.[3] Other scholars reach similar conclusions for different countries: Stephen Van Evera advocates German acquisition of a nuclear arsenal to deter Russia; Barry Posen recommends that Ukraine keep nuclear weapons as a deterrent against future Russian military intervention; Peter Lavoy predicts that nuclear weapons will prevent future wars between India and Pakistan; and both Martin van Creveld and Shai Feldman maintain that nuclear proliferation in the Middle East will stabilize the Arab-Israeli conflict.[4] This "proliferation optimist" position flows easily from the logic of rational deterrence theory: the possession of nuclear weapons by two powers can reduce the likelihood of war precisely because it makes the costs of war so great.

Such optimistic views of the effects of nuclear proliferation have not escaped criticism, of course, and a number of scholars have argued that nuclear deterrence may not be stable in specific regional settings.[5] What is missing in the debate so far, however, is an alternative *theory* of the consequences of nuclear proliferation; an alternative that is a broader conception of the effects of nuclear weapons proliferation on the likelihood of war. In this chapter I present such an alternative, rooted in organization theory, which leads to a far more pessimistic assessment of the future prospects for peace.

There are two central arguments. First, I argue that professional military organizations—because of common biases, inflexible routines, and parochial interests—display organizational behaviors that are likely to lead to deterrence failures and deliberate or accidental war. Unlike the widespread psychological critique of rational deter-

rence theory—which maintains that some political leaders may lack the intelligence or emotional stability to
make deterrence work[6]—this organizational critique argues that military organizations, unless professionally
managed through a checks-and-balances system of strong
civilian control, are unlikely to fulfill the operational requirements for stable nuclear deterrence.

Second, I argue that there are strong reasons to believe that future nuclear-armed states will lack the positive mechanisms of civilian control. Many current and
emerging proliferators have either military-run governments or weak civilian-led governments in which the
professional military has a strong and direct influence on
policymaking. In such states, the biases, routines, and
parochial interests of powerful military organizations,
not the "objective" interests of the state, can determine
state behavior. In addition, military organizations in
many proliferators are "inward-looking," focusing primarily on issues of domestic stability and internal politics, rather than on external threats to national security.
When such militaries are in power, senior officers' ener-
gies and interests necessarily shift away from professional concerns for the protection of national security;
when civilians are in power, but are extremely fearful of
military coups, defense policy is designed to protect their
regime, not the nation's security, and officers are promoted according to their personal loyalty to current leaders, not their professional competence. In either case,
such extensive military involvement in domestic politics,
whether active or latent, means that the military's professional competence as a fighting force, and also as a
manager of a deterrent force, will suffer. Finally, some
new nuclear states have been "born nuclear": Ukraine,
Belarus, and Kazakhstan inherited nuclear weapons from
the Soviet Union without inheriting its stable civil-
military relations, historical learning experience, or extensive command and control mechanisms.

What are the likely effects of the spread of nuclear weapons? My argument proceeds in three steps. First, I contrast the assumptions and logic of proliferation optimists to the assumptions and logic of a more pessimistic organizational-level approach to nuclear proliferation. Next, I compare the two theories' predictions about three major operational requirements of deterrence and, in each case, I present the existing empirical evidence concerning each requirement. Finally, at the end of the chapter, I present some lessons for international relations theory and United States nonproliferation policy.

RATIONAL DETERRENCE THEORY AND ORGANIZATION THEORY COMPARED

Rational Deterrence Theory

The influential writings of Kenneth Waltz are the most clear and confident expressions of faith in rational nuclear deterrence. "Nuclear weapons have been given a bad name," Waltz maintains, "because catastrophic outcomes of nuclear exchanges are easy to imagine, leaders of states will shrink in horror from initiating them. With nuclear weapons, stability and peace rest on easy calculations of what one country can do to another. Anyone—political leader or man in the street—can see that catastrophe lurks if events spiral out of control and nuclear warheads begin to fly."[7] Given that the costs of nuclear war are so high, even a small risk of war can produce strong deterrence. Because "a nation will be deterred from attacking even if it believes that there is only a possibility that its adversary will retaliate," Waltz maintains that "the probability of major war among states having nuclear weapons approaches zero."[8] If this is true, then the spread of nuclear weapons should have very positive consequences: "The likelihood of war decreases as deterrent and defensive capabilities increase. Nuclear weapons make wars hard to start. These statements hold for small as for big nuclear powers. Because they do, the gradual spread of nuclear weapons is more to be welcomed than feared" (Ch. 1, p. 45).

Waltz writes with disdain about what he calls the "ethnocentric views" of psychological critics of deterrence: "Many Westerners write fearfully about a future in which Third World countries have nuclear weapons. They seem to view their people in the old imperial manner as `lesser breeds without the law'" (Ch. 1, p. 13). For nuclear deterrence to work, he argues, one does not need to assume that decisionmakers in new nuclear states make intricate rational calculations about every policy decision: it is sufficient that statesmen are highly "sensitive to costs" (Ch. 1, pp. 12–13), a requirement, Waltz elsewhere acknowledges, "which for convenience can be called an assumption of rationality."[9] When costs are so high, such sensitivity is easy and deterrence is therefore not difficult: "One need not become preoccupied with the characteristics of the state that is to be deterred or scrutinize its leaders," Waltz insists, since "in a nuclear world *any state* will be deterred by another state's second-strike forces."[10]

Within the rational deterrence framework, three major operational requirements for stable nuclear deterrence exist: 1) there must not be a preventive war during the transition period when one state has nuclear weapons and the other state is building, but has not yet achieved, a nuclear capability; 2) both states must develop, not just the ability to inflict some level of unacceptable damage to the other side, but also a sufficient degree of "second-strike" survivability so that its forces could retaliate if attacked first; and 3) the nuclear arsenals must not be prone to accidental or unauthorized use. Nuclear optimists believe that new nuclear powers will meet these requirements because it is in these states' obvious interests to do so. This is, as I will show, a very problematic belief.

An Organizational Perspective

The assumption that states behave in a basically rational manner is of course an assumption, not an empirically tested insight. International relations scholars often assume high degrees of rationality, not because it is accurate, but because it is helpful: it provides a relatively simple way of making predictions, by linking perceived interests with expected behavior. The rational-actor view is clearly not the only one possible, however, and it is not the only set of assumptions that lead to useful predictions about nuclear proliferation.

An alternative set of assumptions views government leaders as intending to behave rationally, yet sees their beliefs, the options available to them, and the final implementation of their decisions as being influenced by powerful forces within the country. If this is the case, organization theory should be useful for the study of the consequences of proliferation. This is important, since such an organizational perspective challenges the central assumption that states behave in a self-interested, rational manner.

Two themes in organization theory focus attention on major impediments to pure rationality in organizational behavior. First, large organizations function within a severely "bounded," or limited, form of rationality: they have inherent limits on calculation and coordination and use simplifying mechanisms to understand and respond to uncertainty in the outside world.[11] Organizations, by necessity, develop routines to coordinate action among different units: standard operating procedures and organizational rules, not individually reasoned decisions, therefore govern behavior. Organizations commonly "satisfice": rather than searching for the policy that maximizes their utility, they often accept the first option that is minimally satisfying. Organizations are often myopic: instead of surveying the entire environment for information, organizational members have biased searches, focusing only on specific areas stemming from their past experience, recent training, and current responsibility. Organizations suffer from "goal displacement": they often become fixated on narrow operational measurements of goals and lose focus on their overall objectives. Organizational filters continually shape the beliefs and actions of individuals. As James March and Herbert Simon put it, "the world tends to be perceived by the organization members in terms of the particular concepts that are reflected in the organization's vocabulary. The particular categories it employs are reified, and become, for members of the organization, attributes of the world rather than mere conventions."[12]

Second, complex organizations commonly have multiple, conflicting goals, and the process by which objectives are chosen and pursued is intensely political.[13] From such a political perspective, actions that cut against the interests of the organization's leadership are often found to serve the narrow interests of some units within the organization. Organizations are not simply tools in the hands of higher-level authorities but are groups of self-interested and competitive subunits and actors. "Theory should see conflict as an inevitable part of organizational life stemming from organizational characteristics rather than from the characteristics of individuals," Charles Perrow has argued. For example, organizational divisions and responsibilities help explain why "sales and production [are] in conflict in all firms . . . or faculty and administration in colleges, doctors and nurses and administrators in hospitals, the treatment and custodial staffs in prisons."[14] This is also true in military organizations: weapon system operators often have different interests than their commanders, units in the field have different interests than the command headquarters, a particular service has different interests than the General Staff or the Joint Chiefs. And even when a professional military service or command acts in relatively rational ways to maximize *its* interests—protecting its power, size, autonomy or organizational essence—such actions do not necessarily reflect the organizational interests of the military as a whole, much less the national interests of the state. To the degree that such narrow organizational interests determine state behavior, a theory of "rational" state action is seriously weakened.

Although organization theory has been highly useful in a number of substantive areas of international relations—illuminating crisis behavior, alliance politics, weapons procurement, military doctrine, and nuclear weapons safety[15]—it has not been used extensively to study the consequences of proliferation. This is unfortunate, since each of the three operational requirements for rational deterrence appear in a different light when viewed from an organizational perspective. What are professional military views about preventive war; could such views influence the probability of a nuclear attack during the transition period of an early arms race? What is the likelihood that professional militaries will develop and deploy survivable nuclear forces to maintain stable deterrence? What is the likely influence of the structures and biases of military organizations on the prevention of accidental and unauthorized uses of nuclear weapons in new proliferating states?

The next section presents predictions and empirical evidence concerning the three operational requirements for stable nuclear deterrence. In each section, I contrast the predictions made by nuclear optimists to the predictions deduced from an organizational approach and then present two kinds of evidence. The evidence from the United States case will be given first, both because there is more evidence available on American nuclear weapons operations and because the United States should be considered a tough test of my organizational approach since it is widely considered to have a highly professionalized military under a strong and institutionalized system of civilian control. If these problems are found to exist in the United States, therefore, they are likely to be even more pronounced in other nations. The currently available evidence about other nuclear states is then presented. Both kinds of evidence provide strong support for my pessimistic conclusion about the consequences of the spread of nuclear weapons.

PREVENTIVE WAR IN THE TRANSITION PERIOD

The first operational requirement of mutual nuclear deterrence between two powers concerns the transition period between a conventional world and a nuclear world: the first state to acquire weapons must not attack its rival now, in a *preventive war*, in order to avoid the risk of a worse war later, after the second state has acquired a large nuclear arsenal.[16] There are two periods in a nuclear arms race, according to Waltz, during which a state might consider a preventive strike: when its rival is developing nuclear capability but has clearly not yet constructed a bomb, and when the rival is in a more advanced state of nuclear development and therefore might have a small number of weapons. Waltz maintains that a preventive strike might seem to make sense "during the first stage of nuclear development [since] a state could strike without fearing that the country it attacked would return a nuclear blow." Yet, he insists that such attacks are unlikely, because it would not be in a state's longer-term interests: "But would one country strike so hard as to destroy another country's potential for future nuclear development? If it did not, the country struck could resume its nuclear career. If the blow struck is less than devastating, one must be prepared either to repeat it or to occupy and control the country. To do either would be forbiddingly difficult" (Ch. 1, p. 18).

Later, once an adversary has developed "even a rudimentary nuclear capability," all rational incentives for preventive war are off, since "one's own severe punishment becomes possible" (Ch. 1, p. 19). A little uncertainty goes a long way in Waltz's world. If there is even a remote chance of nuclear retaliation, a rational decisionmaker will not launch a preventive war.

An organizational perspective, however, leads to a more pessimistic assessment of the likelihood of preventive nuclear wars, because it draws attention to military biases that could encourage such attacks. Waltz has dismissed this argument since he believes that military leaders are *not* more likely than civilians to recommend the use of military force during crises.[17] Although this may be true with respect to cases of military intervention *in general*, there are five strong reasons to expect that military officers are predisposed to view *preventive war in particular* in a much more favorable light than are civilian authorities.

First, military officers, because of self-selection into the profession and socialization afterwards, are more inclined than the rest of the population to see war as likely in the near term and inevitable in the long run.[18] The professional focus of attention on warfare makes military officers skeptical of nonmilitary alternatives to war, while civilian leaders often place stronger hopes on diplomatic and economic methods of long-term conflict resolution. Such beliefs make military officers particularly susceptible to "better now than later" logic. Second, officers are trained to focus on pure military logic, and are given strict operational goals to meet, when addressing security problems. "Victory" means defeating the enemy in a narrow military sense, but does not necessarily mean achieving broader political goals in war, which would include reducing the costs of war to acceptable levels. For military officers, diplomatic, moral, or domestic political costs of preventive war are also less likely to be influential than would be the case for civilian officials. Third, military officers display strong biases in favor of offensive doctrines and decisive operations.[19] Offensive doctrines enable military organizations to take the initiative, utilizing their standard plans under conditions they control, while forcing adversaries to react to their favored strategies. Decisive operations utilize the principle of mass, may reduce casualties, and are more likely to lead to a military decision rather than a political stalemate. Preventive war would clearly have these desired characteristics. Fourth, the military, like most organizations, tends to plan incrementally, leading it to focus on immediate plans for war and not on the subsequent problems of managing the postwar world. Fifth, military officers, like most members of large organizations, focus on their narrow job. Managing the postwar world is the politicians' job, not part of military officers' operational responsibility, and officers are therefore likely to be short-sighted, not examining the long-term political and diplomatic consequences of preventive war. In theory, these five related factors should often make military officers strong advocates of preventive war.

Evidence on Preventive War from the U.S. Case

What differences existed between U.S. civilian and military advice on the use of nuclear weapons during the early Cold War? During major crises, few disagreements emerged. For example, after the Chinese military intervention in the Korean War in late November 1950, both Truman's senior military and civilian advisors recommended against the use of the atomic bomb on the Korean peninsula.[20] If one focuses specifically on the issue of *preventive war*, however, strong differences between civilian and military opinions can be seen. During both the Truman and Eisenhower administrations, senior U.S. military officers seriously advocated preventive-war options and, in both cases, continued favoring such ideas well after civilian leaders ruled against them.

Although U.S. military officers were not alone in recommending preventive war during the Truman administration—as diverse a set of individuals as philosopher Bertrand Russell, mathematician John Von Neumann, and Navy Secretary Francis Matthews called for such a policy—within the government, military leaders were clearly the predominant and most persistent advocates.[21] The Joint Chiefs of Staff (JCS) were quite direct in their advocacy of preventive options, calling for the "readiness and determination to take prompt and effective military action abroad to *anticipate and prevent attack*" in their September 1945 top-secret report on postwar U.S. military policy: "When it becomes evident that forces of aggression are being arrayed against us by a potential enemy, we cannot afford, through any misguided and perilous idea of avoiding an aggressive attitude to permit the first blow to be struck against us."[22] Truman appears to have rejected the whole concept of preventive war rather quickly, however, largely on moral and domestic political grounds. "We do not believe in aggression or preventive war," he announced in a public broadcast in 1950. "Such a war is the weapon of dictators, not of free democratic countries like the United States."[23]

The issue was not thoroughly addressed at the highest levels, however, until April 1950, when NSC-68 (National Security Council Document 68) presented three key arguments against preventive nuclear war. First, intelligence estimates suggested that a U.S. atomic attack on the USSR "would not force or induce the Kremlin to capitulate and that the Kremlin would still be able to use the forces under its control to dominate most or all of Eurasia." Second, a preventive attack "would be repugnant to many Americans" and therefore difficult to justify at home. Third, U.S. allies, especially in Western Europe, would share such beliefs, hurting U.S. relations with them and making it "difficult after such a war to create satisfactory international order." The conclusion was clear: "These considerations are no less weighty because they are imponderable, and they rule out an attack unless it is demonstrably in the nature of a counter-attack to a blow which is on its way or about to be delivered."[24]

Senior military leaders were very cautious about discussing preventive nuclear strikes in public after that, with the exception of Major General Orvil Anderson, the commandant of the Air War College, whom Truman fired in September 1950 for advocating preventive nuclear war to the press.[25] Yet, in private, military support for preventive options remained high. Generals George Kenney, Curtis LeMay, Thomas Power, Nathan Twining, Thomas White, and Hoyt Vandenberg all privately expressed sympathy for preventive nuclear war and official air force doctrine manuals continued to support preventive-war ideas.[26]

More open discussions of preventive-war options reemerged at the highest levels of the U.S. government during the first two years of the Eisenhower administration. Throughout the new administration's reevaluation of U.S. security strategy, senior military officers again supported preventive options. The U.S. Air War College, for example, produced the extensive "Project Control" study in 1953 and 1954, which advocated preventive war if necessary.[27] This study called for taking direct control of Soviet airspace and threatening massive bombing unless the Kremlin agreed to an ultimatum to withdraw troops from Eastern Europe, dissolve the Cominform, and abandon the Sino-Soviet alliance. Project Control was greeted with enthusiasm when it was briefed to Chairman of the Joint Chiefs of Staff (JCS) Admiral Arthur Radford in July 1954, though State Department officials complained that such schemes were "simply another version of preventive war."[28] In addition, Eisenhower himself was briefed on a JCS Advanced Study Group report in mid-1954 which, according to a contemporary memorandum on the report, "pointed unmistakably to an advocacy of the US deliberately precipitating war with the USSR in the near future—that is before the USSR could achieve a large enough thermo-nuclear capability to be a real menace to the Continental US."[29]

The most extreme preventive-war arguments by a senior officer, however, can be found in General Twining's August 1953 memorandum to the JCS on "The Coming National Crisis," which would occur, he maintained, when the USSR developed sufficient nuclear forces so that "our military establishment would be unable to insure the survival of our nation":

> Prior to entering the second period of time [when the Soviet Union could destroy the U.S.] if our objectives have not been achieved by means short of general war, it will be necessary to adopt other measures. We must recognize this time of decision, or, we will continue blindly down a suicidal path and arrive at a situation in which we will have entrusted our survival to the whims of a small group of proven barbarians. If we believe it unsafe, unwise, or immoral to gamble that the enemy will tolerate our existence under this circumstance, we must be militarily prepared to support such decisions as might involve general war.[30]

The Joint Chiefs final position was much more calm in tone, though it too displayed "better now than later" logic. While acknowledging that official U.S. policy prohibited preventive war, Admiral Radford told the National Security Council in November 1954 that "if we continue to pursue a policy of simply reacting to Communist initiatives, instead of a policy of forestalling Communist action, we cannot hope for anything but a showdown with Soviet Communists by 1959 or 1960," adding ominously that the JCS could "guarantee" a successful outcome in a nuclear war only if it occurred "prior to Soviet achievement of atomic plenty."[31]

Why did Eisenhower reject this line of thinking? Eisenhower clearly did not object to preventive war on moral grounds.[32] Instead, his eventual rejection of preventive war appears to have been determined by his increasing belief that a preventive nuclear attack on the USSR would be too costly politically, *even if it succeeded* in narrow military terms. The political and human costs of maintaining control over a decimated Soviet society were especially appalling to Eisenhower. As he told a group of officers in June 1954:

> No matter how well prepared for war we may be, no matter how certain we are that within 24 hours we could destroy Kuibyshev and Moscow and Leningrad and Baku and all the other places that would allow the Soviets to carry on war, I want you to carry this question home with you: Gain such a victory, and what do you do with it? Here would be a great area from the Elbe to Vladivostok and down through Southeast Asia torn up and destroyed without government, without its communications, just an area of starvation and disaster. I ask you what would the civilized world do about it? I repeat there is no victory in any war except through our imaginations, through our dedication, and through our work to avoid it.[33]

Preventive War among New Nuclear States

This evidence presented here does *not* demonstrate that the United States almost launched a preventive war on the USSR in the early Cold War period. Nor do I mean to suggest that civilian leaders could never rationally choose to launch a preventive attack. This evidence does strongly suggest, however, that military officers have strong proclivities in favor of preventive war and that proliferation optimists are therefore wrong to assume that *any* leader of a state will automatically be deterred by an adversary's "rudimentary" arsenal, or even by a significantly larger one. Preventive nuclear attacks were clearly imagined, actively planned, and vigorously advocated by senior U.S. military leaders well beyond the initial development and deployment of nuclear weapons by the USSR.[34] Without Truman's and Eisenhower's broader mix of moral and political objections to preventive war, the narrow military logic in favor of such an option might have prevailed.[35]

The "better now than later" logic of preventive war is likely to be under serious consideration whenever an existing nuclear power sees a rival developing a nuclear arsenal. Preventive war is more likely to be chosen, however, if military leaders have a significant degree of direct or indirect influence over the final decision. While there have not yet been any nuclear preventive wars among the new nuclear states, the probability of such attacks will increase since civilian control over the military is more problematic in many of these states.

Pakistan is the most dramatic case in point, since a rapid development of a Pakistani operational nuclear arsenal could create a temporary nuclear superiority over India, which reportedly refrained from building an arsenal after its 1974 nuclear test.[36] Military biases in favor of preventive war have been highly influential in the past in Pakistan, where the military has been in direct control of the government for more than half of the state's history. Pakistani military leaders have repeatedly advocated and initiated preventive war against India. In the fall of 1962, senior military authorities unsuccessfully urged President Mohammed Ayub Khan, the leader of the military-controlled government, to attack India while its army was tied down in the conflict with China.[37]

Three years later, in September 1965, the Ayub government did launch a preventive war on India in an effort to conquer Kashmir before the anticipated Indian military build-up was completed.[38] The Pakistani attack on India in December 1971 was also strongly influenced by the parochial organizational interests of senior army and air force leaders since, as Richard Sisson and Leo Rose have stressed, the ruling military viewed threats to Bengal as "threats to their image, threats to the welfare of the military in a successor state, and threats in the way of charges that the military was prepared to barter away Pakistani sovereignty."[39] Finally, in May 1990, at least some members of the U.S. intelligence community believed that the Pakistan Air Force took initial nuclear alerting actions during the crisis over Kashmir. The reports—which include claims that nuclear weapons were assembled, taken out of storage sites, and loaded onto Pakistani F-16 aircraft—are alarming, not only because of the potential for nuclear escalation, but also because Pakistani Prime Minister Benazir Bhutto was reportedly not kept informed of Pakistan's military activities by her senior officers during the crisis.[40] Later in 1990, the Bhutto regime was ousted by the Pakistan military, after she attempted to push her own loyal candidate into the army chief of staff position. Despite Bhutto's later return to power, unfortunately, there is little reason to assume that future Pakistani governments, even if nominally democratic in nature, will be entirely resistant to such parochial military pressures.

The possible maintenance of a nuclear arsenal by Ukraine is a second example that should raise fears of the possibility of preventive war. (The Ukraine government has promised to return the thousands of nuclear weapons on its soil to dismantlement plants in Russia, but a lot can happen before the final shipments are made, and some officials and legislators in Kiev advocate that Ukraine renege on this commitment and keep a moderate-size nuclear arsenal for its defense.) From a broad organizational perspective, it is very worrisome that Ukraine has yet to develop stable civil-military relations and that Ukrainian military officers, alarmed over their loss of status and decreasing living standards, have repeatedly threatened "to resort to extreme measures" if their social demands are not satisfied.[41] Given the vast Russian military superiority over Ukraine, however, the great uncertainty about future Russian civil-military relations is also alarming. Soon after the breakup of the Soviet Union, Russian papers reported that Russian President Boris Yeltsin privately discussed the idea of a "preventive nuclear strike" against Ukraine, but ruled against any such attack.[42] Nevertheless, the nuclear war plans drafted by Russian military planners reportedly include first-strike options against the nuclear forces in Ukraine.[43] If future Russian-Ukrainian relations ever deteriorate to the point where armed conflict is seriously considered, military pressure on the Russian government to attack any nuclear weapons remaining in the Ukraine, before they could be readied for possible use by the Kiev government, could be significant.

Nuclear optimists dismiss this possibility. Ukrainian weapons will enhance deterrence, they argue, but not increase the risk of preventive war. For example, John Mearsheimer maintains that "military calculations alone should suffice to deter the Russians from launching a preventive war". "The probability of Ukrainian nuclear retaliation would be small, but the Russians could never be sure that Ukraine would not launch some nuclear weapons back at them, causing cataclysmic damage, even if the retaliation was ragged."[44] Barry Posen is similarly sanguine about what would occur if the Ukrainians tried to seize full operational control over all the nuclear weapons on their soil: "This would be a novel kind of nuclear crisis, but it would probably be enough of a crisis to produce the prudent behavior among nuclear powers that existed during the Cold War."[45]

Leaving aside the question of whether the superpowers always exhibited "prudent behavior" in Cold War crises, there are several reasons to be concerned about whether a future Russian government would be deterred from preventive attacks under all circumstances. First, because of its previous custody of the Soviet arsenal, Moscow would know the normal locations of Ukrainian weapons and the operational details of their alerting procedures and command and control networks. Second, the evidence from the only historical precedent—the discussions held in Moscow in 1969 on whether to launch a preventive strike on Chinese nuclear forces—is hardly reassuring, since the minister of defense reportedly favored a preventive attack despite the existence of a small Chinese nuclear arsenal at that time. Organizational preparations for a possible strike went as far as a countrywide air force alert and military exercises, including mock bombing runs against targets designed to resemble Chinese nuclear facilities. The Politburo, however, did not approve of an attack, in part because the United States made it clear that it would strongly oppose such action.[46] Third, the strength of civilian control of the Russian military has been severely challenged since the breakup of the USSR.[47] For example, Russian military units in the break-away "Transdniestr Republic" and in Georgia have repeatedly intervened in the conflicts there, reportedly without explicit permission from the civilian leadership in Moscow, and President Yeltsin later revealed that senior Russian generals did not follow his direct orders during the domestic political crisis of October 1993.[48] If the democratic reform movement fails in post–Cold War Russia, and senior military officers continue to enter the political arena in a conservative successor government, their political influence would grow even greater. A likely consequence is more direct military influence on major foreign policy decisions, including future decisions about preventive war in crises.

Other states with unstable civil-military relations could get nuclear weapons in the future. I cannot predict the exact strength of such preventive-war pressures or the timing of serious threats of war between all future nuclear states. Nevertheless, because civilians will not be in firm control in all future nuclear states, there are good reasons to fear that military biases in favor of preventive war will be more likely to prevail than was the case with the superpowers during the Cold War.

INTERESTS, ROUTINES, AND SURVIVABLE FORCES

The second operational requirement of deterrence is that new nuclear powers must build invulnerable second-strike nuclear forces. The United States and the former Soviet Union developed a large and diverse arsenal—long-range bombers, intercontinental ballistic missiles, cruise missiles, and submarine-launched missiles—and a complex network of satellite and radar warning systems, to decrease the risks of a successful first strike against their arsenals. Will new nuclear powers also construct invulnerable arsenals? How quickly?

Waltz addresses this issue with two related arguments. First, only a very small number of nuclear weapons are necessary for successful deterrence: since each nuclear warhead contains so much destructive power, "not much is required to deter"(Ch.1, p. 22). Second, no rational nuclear power would permit all of its forces to be vulnerable to an enemy first strike. According to Waltz, "Nuclear forces are seldom delicate because no state wants delicate forces, and nuclear forces can easily be made sturdy. Nuclear weapons can be fairly small and light, and they are easy to hide and to move" (Ch. 1, p.

19). In short, Waltz is confident that any state will create the minimum deterrent of an invulnerable second-strike nuclear arsenal. "Because so much explosive power comes in such small packages, the invulnerability of a sufficient number of warheads is easy to achieve and the delivery of fairly large numbers of warheads impossible to thwart, both now and as far into the future as anyone can see."[49]

It is puzzling, however, for a theory that emphasizes the rationality of actors, to note that both superpowers during the Cold War believed that they needed much larger forces than the minimum deterrence requirement. Waltz insists, however, that that belief was the result of "decades of fuzzy thinking" about nuclear deterrence: "The two principal powers in the system have long had second-strike forces, with neither able to launch a disarming strike against the other. That both nevertheless continue to pile weapon upon unneeded weapon is a puzzle whose solution can be found only within the United States and the Soviet Union."[50] Yet, if "fuzzy thinking" at the domestic level can cause a state to spend billions of dollars building more forces than are necessary for rational deterrence, couldn't similar "fuzzy thinking" at the organizational level of analysis also lead a state to build inadequate forces?

Why would professional militaries *not* develop invulnerable nuclear forces if left to their own devices? Four reasons emerge from the logic of organizational theory. First, military bureaucracies, like other organizations, are usually interested in having more resources: they want more weapons, more men in uniform, more pieces of the budget pie. This could obviously lead to larger than necessary nuclear arsenals. Yet programs for making nuclear arsenals less vulnerable to attack (for example building concrete shelters or missile-carrying trains) are very expensive, and therefore *decrease* the re-

sources available for the military hardware, the missiles
or aircraft, that the organization values most highly. Military biases can therefore lead to more weapons but not
necessarily more survivable weapons. Second, militaries,
like other organizations, have favored traditional ways of
doing things and therefore maintain a strong sense of
organizational "essence."[51] Since eforts to decrease the
vulnerability of nuclear forces often require new missions
and weapon systems—and, indeed, often new organizational units—one would expect that the existing organizations would be resistant. Third, if organizational plans
for war and conceptions of deterrence do not require invulnerable forces, they will not have incentives to pursue
building them. Thus, if military officers believe that they
are likely to engage in preventive war, preemptive attacks, or even launch-on-warning options, then survivability measures may be simply perceived as unnecessary. Fourth, military organizations inevitably develop
routines to coordinate actions among numerous individuals and subunits, and such routines are commonly
inflexible and slow to change. Even if the technical requirements for invulnerability exist, however, poorly designed standard operating procedures and military routines can undermine a survivable military force.

Evidence from the U.S. Case

The history of U.S. nuclear weapons programs strongly
supports these organizational arguments. The United
States eventually developed invulnerable second-strike
forces, but only after civilian authorities forced reluctant
military organizations to deploy new weapons systems
and change traditional operational practices. The influence of such factors can be seen in the history of three
major weapons developments: the creation of a survivable basing system for strategic bombers in the United
States; the development of the submarine-launched bal-

listic missile (SLBM); and the construction of the inter-continental-range ballistic missile (ICBM).

The first case in point is the development of a survivable basing system for Strategic Air Command (SAC) bombers in the mid-1950s. SAC war plans at the time—based on routines developed during World War II when the air force had not faced threats of air strikes against their long-range bomber bases—called for sending the nuclear retaliatory force to bases on the periphery of the Soviet Union in crises.[52] These overseas bases, however, became highly vulnerable to a surprise Soviet first strike, and, making matters even worse, air force regulations required SAC to concentrate the facilities at individual bases to minimize the peacetime costs of utilities, pipelines, and roads. When civilian analysts at the RAND Corporation pointed out the ill-wisdom of such plans, narrow organizational interests produced significant resistance to change. SAC's autonomy was threatened: officers there feared that the RAND study would lead to broader interference in SAC operations. Moreover, as Bruce Smith put it, SAC officers feared that "the Air Force could also be embarrassed before Congress" and that "the study could undermine the confidence and morale of their units."[53] The basing study led to radical changes in SAC operational plans, including U.S. basing and in-flight refueling, only after independent civilian RAND analysts did a successful "end-run" around the system, bypassing layers of opposition in SAC and briefing senior air force leaders directly.[54]

The U.S. SLBM force has been the least vulnerable component of the strategic arsenal for over thirty years, yet it is important to note that this weapons system was developed *against* the wishes of the U.S. Navy leadership. The major impediment to development of the Polaris missile system was, as Harvey Sapolsky notes, "the Navy's indecisiveness about sponsoring a ballistic missile program."[55] Senior naval officers were concerned in the early 1950s that, given the Eisenhower administration's budget cuts, spending on missile programs would come at the expense of more traditional navy programs and insisted that the Strategic Air Command should pay for sea-based missiles. Even navy submariners were unenthusiastic since "in their view, submarines were meant to sink ships with torpedoes, not to blast land targets with missiles"[56] The program's supporters within the navy eventually were forced to go to a group of civilian outsiders, the Killian Committee, to get endorsement of the program.[57] Without continued high-level civilian intervention, it is not clear whether or when a large-scale SLBM force would have been constructed.

Similar organizational resistance to innovation can be observed in the early history of the ICBM force. Why did the U.S. Air Force take so long to develop strategic missiles, eventually producing the perceived missile gap crisis? In his compelling study of the missile program, Edmund Beard concludes that "the United States could have developed an ICBM considerably earlier than it did but that such development was hindered by organizational structures and belief patterns that did not permit it."[58] Devotion to manned aircraft, and especially the manned bomber, led to a prolonged period of neglect for ICBM research and development funds. As late as 1956, General Curtis LeMay placed the ICBM as the air force's sixth-highest priority weapon, with four new aircraft and a cruise-missile program above it; and even within the air force's guided missile branch, air-to-air and air-to-surface missiles (which were to be used to help bombers penetrate to their targets) were given higher priority than intercontinental-range surface-to-surface missiles.[59] Again, civilian intervention was critical: not until the Killian Committee report recommended that ICBMs also be made a national priority, and civilian Pentagon officials threatened to create a separate agency to oversee the program, did the air force put adequate funds into ICBM development.[60]

Will New Nuclear Powers Build Survivable Forces?

This evidence demonstrates that there are strong organizational reasons to expect that professional militaries, if left on their own, may not construct an invulnerable nuclear arsenal. Logic would therefore lead to a prediction that the development of a secure retaliatory force would be especially prolonged in time and imperfect in implementation in states in which civilian control over military organizations is problematic. Although these organizational impediments are likely to take somewhat different forms in different states, evidence does exist suggesting that parochial organizational interests and rigid routines have impeded the development of secure retaliatory forces in the developing world.

The influence of organizational biases on strategic weapons deployments can perhaps best be seen in the People's Republic of China. China tested its first nuclear weapon in 1964, yet it did not develop a confident and secure second-strike capability until the early 1980s, when initial deployments of ICBMs (1981), SLBMs (1982–83), and mobile and concealed IRBMs were instituted (1980).[61] Why did China, which developed the atomic and hydrogen bombs very quickly, take so long to develop invulnerable missile-basing modes? The absence of perceived strategic threats is not a plausible answer, since the clashes along the Sino-Soviet border and the subsequent nuclear threats from Moscow occurred in 1969. Indeed, in 1970, U.S. intelligence agencies predicted that China would deploy ICBMs by 1975; and the failure to do so promptly has been described as "a major enigma in the PRC's strategic weapons effort."[62]

While both technical problems and the political turmoil of the Cultural Revolution clearly played roles in the delayed development of Chinese strategic missiles, professional military biases also had an apparent impact in two specific areas. First, it is important to note that the military officers of Second Artillery Division, who controlled the operational missile forces in the 1970s, consistently argued for larger arsenals, but did not independently pursue the survivability measures needed for the existing land-based missiles. Only in 1975, after Mao Zedong approved a weapons institute report recommending that advanced deception measures be used to make China's medium-range ballistic missiles less vulnerable to Soviet attacks, were successful camouflage and cave-basing deployment methods developed.[63] As was the case in the United States, high-level intervention by civilian authorities was necessary to encourage operational innovation. Second, the strong bureaucratic power of traditional People's Liberation Army interests in the party and weapons institutes appears to have slowed the development of the Chinese navy's SLBM force. The SLBM and ICBM programs were started at the same time, but land-based systems were consistently given higher priority: the reverse engineering of SLBM missiles supplied by the Soviets was abandoned in 1961, while similar land-based missile programs continued; and in the late 1960s, the DF [ICBM] program was considered a "crash effort," while "the JL-1 [SLBM] designers did not feel an immediate or compelling urgency."[64] Thus, while China eventually developed a diverse set of survivable forces, it was a very vulnerable nuclear power for a longer period of time than can be explained by the rationalist assumptions of proliferation optimists.

Even if apparently invulnerable forces are built, however, their ability to withstand a first strike will be highly problematic if inappropriate organizational practices and operational routines are maintained. I will provide two examples. A useful illustration of how poorly designed organizational procedures and routines can produce "unnecessary" force vulnerabilities can be seen in Egyptian air force operations in June 1967. Given the balance between the Egyptian and Israeli air forces at the time (Egypt had over a 2-to-1 advantage in bombers, fighter-bombers, and interceptors[65]), Egyptian authorities had strong reasons to believe that their ability to retaliate against any Israeli air attack was secure. Indeed, President Nasser publicly emphasized that the Israeli "fear of the Egyptian air force and bombers" was a deterrent to war, when he ordered that the Gulf of Aqaba be closed.[66] Two organizational routines of the Egyptian Air Force, however, created a severe vulnerability for what was "objectively" a sufficient retaliatory force. First, during the crisis, the air force lined up most of its aircraft wing-tip to wing-tip on the runways, making them easier to launch in a first strike, rather than dispersing them to reduce their vulnerability to an Israeli attack.[67] Second, the Egyptians always placed an interceptor force into defensive air patrol positions and held a "stand-to" alert at air bases at dawn, when they believed an Israeli strike was most likely. Both these operations routinely ended at 7:30 A.M., and, having observed these organizational practices, the Israelis attacked at 7:45 when the planes had landed for refueling and the pilots and crews were having breakfast.[68] What appeared to be an invulnerable force was thus virtually destroyed in the first hours of the war.

A second example concerns North Korea. If the North Korean government moves forward with its nuclear weapons program, in violation of international agreements, will it build a survivable deterrent force, successfully hiding the weapons from all potential adversaries? Possibly. But the fact that the North Korean government could not hide its secret nuclear weapons program from its adversaries does not bode well. Even in a highly secretive and centralized system, like the North Korean government, large organizations undertaking complex tasks will follow rules and develop routines that can create inadvertent vulnerabilities. How did the United States come to suspect that North Korea was developing nuclear weapons in violation of the nuclear Non-Proliferation Treaty? Although the full details are shrouded in secrecy, it appears that inappropriate organizational routines were a critical factor. In the early 1990s, the North Korean leadership apparently sought to hide nuclear-waste materials at the Yongbyon reactor facility, evidence that could serve as a tip-off that they were in the process of developing nuclear weapons. The North Koreans, however, were trained by Soviet technical personnel and mimicked the designs of Soviet nuclear-waste storage facilities so closely that U.S. intelligence agencies could immediately identify the covert sites. According to David Albright, "these sites have a distinctive pattern of round and square holes in an above-ground concrete structure that holds liquid and solid waste."[69] This kind of organizational problem— building a covert site following a distinctive pattern developed while constructing earlier sites that were not hidden—is not uncommon. (In 1962, for example, the Russians constructed the secret missile sites in Cuba with a distinctive "four-slash 'signature'" on the concrete revetment, following a routine construction pattern that U.S. intelligence analysts had observed in open missile sites inside the Soviet Union.)[70] In the deadly cat-and-mouse game between nuclear forces and enemy intelligence agencies, such routinized behavior can inadvertently produce a high degree of military vulnerability.

From a purely rationalist perspective, the spread of nuclear weapons to very small powers might be worrisome since such states might not have the financial resources to procure hardened ICBMs or ballistic missile submarines nor sufficient territory to deploy mobile missiles. Awareness of organizational problems, how ever, leads to an even more pessimistic appraisal. Even if the economic resources and geographical conditions for survivable forces exist, a state may not develop a secure second-strike capability if organizational biases and inflexible routines of the professional military dominate its behavior.

ORGANIZATIONS, ACCIDENTS, AND PROLIFERATION

The final operational requirement for stable deterrence is that nuclear arsenals not be prone to accidental or unauthorized use. Waltz believes that any such dangers are temporary and can be easily fixed:

> All nuclear countries live through a time when their forces are crudely designed. All countries have so far been able to control them. Relations between the United States and the Soviet Union, and later among the United States, the Soviet Union, and China, were at their bitterest just when their nuclear forces were in early stages of development and were unbalanced, crude, and presumably hard to control. Why should we expect new nuclear states to experience greater difficulties than the ones old nuclear states were able to cope with? (Ch. 1, pp. 20–21)

Waltz answers his own rhetorical question with a rationalist assumption. It is presumably in the interests of proliferating states to keep their forces under strict control; therefore, they will do so. As he puts it:

> We do not have to wonder whether they will take good care of their weapons. They have every incentive to do so. They will not want to risk retaliation because one or more of their warheads accidentally struck another country. (Ch. 1, p. 21)

What does organization theory say about the likelihood of nuclear weapons accidents? If one assumes that organizations are highly rational, then they might be able to achieve extremely high reliability in managing hazardous technologies, avoiding serious accidents by following three basic strategies: construct highly redundant systems with numerous back-up safety devices; use trial-and-error learning to fix organizational problems after they emerge; and develop a "culture of reliability" through strong socialization and discipline of the organization's members.[71] If one assumes that organizations are only "boundedly" rational and that they contain political conflicts over goals and rewards, however, then a far more pessimistic appraisal is warranted. This approach raises doubts about whether any state can build a large nuclear arsenal that is completely "secure from accident," even if such strategies are followed.

Charles Perrow's *Normal Accidents* argues there are inherent limits to the degree to which any large organization can understand the technical systems it creates to manage hazardous technologies, such as nuclear power plants, petrochemical industries, advanced biotechnology, and oil tankers.[72] If organizations were omniscient, they could anticipate all potential failure modes in their systems and fix them ahead of time. Perrow argues, however, that boundedly rational organizations in the real world will inevitably have serious system accidents over time whenever they exhibit two structural characteristics: high *interactive complexity* (systems containing numerous interrelated, yet unplanned, interactions that are not readily comprehensible) and *tight coupling* (systems with highly time-dependent and invariant production sequences, with limited built-in slack).

My own book, *The Limits of Safety*, adds an explicitly political dimension to "normal accidents theory," which combines with Perrow's structural arguments to produce even greater pessimism about the likelihood of organizational accidents. Conflicting objectives inevitably exist inside any large organization that manages hazardous technology: top-level authorities may place a high priority on safety, but others may place a higher value on more parochial objectives, such as increasing production levels, enhancing the size of their subunit, or promoting their individual careers, which can lead to risky behaviors. Such a focus on the political manner in which conflicting goals are chosen and pursued is necessary to explain both why systems with such dangerous structural characteristics are constructed and why organizational learning about safety problems is often severely limited.[73]

Normal accidents theory suggests that each of the three basic strategies used to improve organizational safety is highly problematic. In some conditions, adding redundant back-up systems can be very counterproductive: redundancy makes the system both more complex and more opaque and therefore can create hidden catastrophic common-mode errors. Large organizations nevertheless often continue to add layers of redundancy upon redundancy to complex systems.[74] Why? Organizations often add redundancy not only when it is needed to improve reliability but also because they must appear to be doing something to solve problems after accidents occur. Unproductive redundancy is also sometimes constructed because such redundant systems serve the narrow interests of organizational subunits, when it enhances *their* size, resources, and autonomy. The politics of blame inside organizations also reduces trial-and-error learning from accidents because organizational leaders have great incentives to find operators at lower levels at fault: this absolves higher leaders from responsibility, and, moreover, it is usually cheaper to fire the operator than to change accident-prone procedures or structures. Knowing this, however, field-level operators have strong incentives not to report safety incidents whenever possible. Finally, from a normal accidents perspective, strong culture and socialization can have negative effects on organizational reliability since they encourage excessive concern about the organization's reputation, disdain for outsiders' and internal dissenters' opinions, and even organizational cover-ups.

The U.S. Nuclear Safety Experience

From the perspective of normal accidents theory, there are strong reasons to expect that the safety of modern nuclear arsenals is inherently limited: large-scale arsenals and command systems are highly complex, by necessity, and are tightly-coupled, by design, to ensure prompt retaliation under attack; the military organizations that manage them are inevitably politicized, with numerous conflicting interests existing between commands and the broader society and within the organizations themselves. How serious were the dangers of U.S. nuclear weapons accidents and even accidental war during the Cold War? The available evidence now demonstrates that there were many more near-accidents than previously recognized. Moreover, the U.S. military's reaction to these safety problems shows how only limited degrees of organizational learning took place.

New information on dangerous military operations during the October 1962 Cuban missile crisis demonstrates these points. At the start of the crisis, the Strategic Air Command secretly deployed nuclear warheads on nine of the ten test ICBMs in place at Vandenberg Air Force Base and then launched the tenth missile, on a prescheduled ICBM test, over the Pacific. No one within the responsible organizations thought through the risks that Soviet intelligence might learn of the nuclear weapons deployment and the alert at Vandenberg and then, in the tension of the crisis, might misinterpret a missile launch from that base. A second safety problem occurred at Malmstrom Air Force Base in Montana at the height of the crisis, when officers jerry-rigged their Minuteman missiles to give themselves the independent ability to launch missiles immediately. This was a serious violation of the Minuteman safety rules, but when an investigation took place after the crisis, the evidence was altered to prevent higher authorities from learning that officers had given themselves the ability to launch unauthorized missile attacks. A third incident occurred on October 28, when the North American Air Defense Command (NORAD) was informed that a nuclear-armed missile had been launched from Cuba and was about to hit Tampa, Florida. Only after the expected detonation failed to occur was it discovered that a radar operator had inserted a test tape simulating an attack from Cuba into the system, confusing control room officers who thought the simulation was a real attack.

Learning from these incidents was minimal: the relevant military procedures and routines were *not* altered after each of these incidents. In each case, the existence of serious safety problems was not reported to or was not recognized by higher authorities. Each one of the accident-prone nuclear operations was therefore repeated by U.S. military commands in October 1973, during the brief U.S. nuclear alert during the Arab-Israeli war.

The history of SAC's B-52 monitor mission at Thule, Greenland, provides a useful example of how adding redundant safety devices to a complex system can inadvertently cause the accidents they are designed to prevent. The U.S. responded to the Soviet development of an ICBM force in the late 1950s by building the Ballistic Missile Early Warning System (BMEWS) radars and developing plans to launch the vulnerable strategic bomber force upon warning. SAC, however, faced a serious problem: if the radar links went dead, would it mean that communications had failed or that a Soviet nuclear attack had started? To make sure that such ambiguity was clarified, NORAD placed radio-equipped "bomb alarm" sensors at the Thule BMEWS base. Yet, SAC wanted to be absolutely sure that it got accurate warning (and wanted to control the means of that warning itself), and therefore also placed a B-52 bomber in a continual orbit over the Thule base, where it could determine whether or not a Soviet attack had begun. The bombers on what became a routine monitor mission were, however, part of the airborne alert force and therefore had thermonuclear weapons on board. No one in the Pentagon or SAC headquarters imagined the possibility that the plane might crash and that an accidental detonation would occur, which would have produced false confirming evidence that a Soviet nuclear attack had occurred.[75] The risks of such an accident were not negligible, however, and even after a series of B-52 bomber crashes led civilians to cancel the airborne alert program in 1968, SAC continued to plan to fly nuclear-armed B-52s above the Thule BMEWS base in future crises.

Proliferation and Nuclear Weapons Safety

Waltz asked why should we expect new nuclear states to experience greater difficulties than did the old ones? The evidence of the number of near-accidents with U.S. nuclear weapons during the Cold War suggests that there would be reason enough to worry about nuclear accidents in new nuclear states even if their safety difficulties were "only" as great as those experienced by old nuclear powers. Unfortunately, there are also six strong reasons to expect that new nuclear states will face even greater risks of nuclear accidents.

First, some emergent nuclear powers lack the organizational and financial resources to produce adequate mechanical safety devices and safe weapons design features. Although all countries may start with "crude nuclear arsenals," in Waltz's terms, the weapons of poorer states will likely be more crude, and will remain so for a longer period of time. Evidence for this prediction can be found in the case of the Iraqi nuclear weapons program, as United Nations' inspectors discovered soon after the 1991 Persian Gulf War:

> The inspectors found out one other thing about the Iraqi bomb [design]— it is highly unstable. The design calls for cramming so much weapon-grade uranium into the core, they say, that the bomb would inevitably be on the verge of going off—even while sitting on the workbench. "It could go off if a rifle bullet hit it," one inspector says, adding: "I wouldn't want to be around if it fell off the edge of this desk."[76]

Second, the "opaque" (or covert) nature of nuclear proliferation in the contemporary world exacerbates nuclear weapons safety problems. Fearing the international diplomatic consequences of a public crossing of the nuclear threshold, most new proliferants have developed weapons capabilities in a secret manner. Israel, India, South Africa, Pakistan, and possibly now North Korea fit this pattern. There are, however, both organizational and technical reasons to believe that this opaque path to nuclear weapons status is inherently less safe.[77] Organizationally, the secrecy and tight compartmentalization of such programs suggests that there will not be thorough monitoring of safety efforts, and the lack of public debate about nuclear issues in such states increases the likelihood that narrow bureaucratic and military interests will not be challenged. (For example, even in the case of India—a very democratic state, but also an undeclared nuclear power—the nuclear weapons complex is not closely monitored and supervised by political leaders.[78]) Finally, an important technical constraint exacerbates the safety problem in such states: the inability to have full-scale nuclear weapons tests hinders the development of effective safety designs.

Third, accident-prone nuclear operations will be more prevalent in states with volatile civil-military relations because military officers, who have organizational biases in favor of maintaining high readiness for war, will be less constrained by more safety-conscious civilian authorities. Pakistan is the most worrisome case in point. The Pakistan air force apparently plans to use U.S. F-16 aircraft in nuclear weapons delivery roles, if necessary in a war. In 1992, however, the U.S. director of Central Intelligence suggested that Pakistan had not perfected the electrical mechanisms to permit safe maintenance, transportation, and delivery of weapons by F-16s.[79] The existence of such safety problems makes the reports that the Pakistani air force may have loaded nuclear weapons on its F-16 aircraft, without informing Prime Minister Bhutto, during the 1990 Kashmir crisis even more alarming than previously recognized.

The fourth reason why new nuclear states will be accident prone is that their tight-coupling problem will be significantly worse at the beginning of the experience with nuclear weapons, since they are in closer proximity to their expected adversaries than was the case between the United States and the Soviet Union. At the start of the Cold War, the superpowers had many hours to determine whether warnings were real or false during the strategic bomber era; later, in the 1960s, they had approximately thirty minutes to react to reports of ICBM attacks; and only after many years of experience with nuclear arsenals did they have to face less than ten minutes of warning time, once missile submarines were deployed off each other's coasts in the 1970s. New and potential future nuclear rivals—Russia and Ukraine, India and Pakistan, North and South Korea—will immediately have very small margins of error at the outset of nuclear rivalries, since they have contiguous borders with their adversaries. Moreover, the poorer of these states are likely to have less reliable warning systems trying to operate successfully in this more challenging environment.

Fifth, although organizational learning about safe nuclear weapons operations was far from perfect in the United States and the Soviet Union during the Cold War, it is likely to be even worse in states that inherited a full-scale nuclear arsenal without going through the incremental learning process of tests, training exercises, and deployments. For example, the emerging problems of nuclear safety in the Ukraine appear to be the product of its unusual status as an "instant" nuclear power. According to Moscow government announcements and press reports, safety problems at Ukrainian military bases have included increased radiation levels at nuclear storage sites, violations of the schedules for technical servicing of missile warheads, defective security and alarm systems at missile silos, violations of nuclear weapons transportation rules, and excessive numbers of warheads being kept in storage facilities.[80] In October 1993, Colonel General Yevgeny Maslin, chief of the Russian General Staff's nuclear ammunition department, reported that two nuclear warheads, which were emitting dangerous levels of radioactivity, had been kept for two weeks inside a railroad car on the Ukraine-Russian border, because Ukrainian custom officials demanded payment for any nuclear weapons taken to Russia for dismantlement.[81] Such nuclear safety problems are dramatic signs of the increased dangers of nuclear weapons accidents that will emerge in any successor republic that keeps weapons inherited from the USSR. Even if the Ukraine, Belarus, and Kazakhstan do eventually disarm under international agreements, the dangers could well be repeated in Russian republics that have strong nationalist and separatist movements, some of which (like Tartarstan) maintain hundreds of nuclear weapons on their soil.[82]

The sixth reason to anticipate a significant increase

in the risks of accidental and unauthorized weapons
detonations is that serious political and social unrest is
likely in the future in a number of these nuclear states.
Waltz, in contrast, insists that domestic instability in new
nuclear powers will not cause serious problems:

> A nuclear state may be unstable or may become so.
> But what is hard to comprehend is why, in an internal
> struggle for power, the contenders would start using
> nuclear weapons. Who would they aim at? . . . One or
> another nuclear state will experience uncertainty of
> succession, fierce struggles for power, and instability
> of regime. Those who fear the worst have not shown
> how those events might lead to the use of nuclear
> weapons. (Ch. 1, p. 10)

This exclusive focus on *deliberate* uses of nuclear
weapons is misleading, however, since severe domestic
instability can produce *accidental* detonations under many
plausible scenarios. If a civil war in a new nuclear state
leads to a fire fight between rival military factions at a
nuclear weapons base, the danger of an accidental detonation or spreading of plutonium would increase. If domestic unrest leads to severe economic hardships at military bases, disgruntled operators are more likely to engage in acts of sabotage that could inadvertently or deliberately produce accidents. An example of the type of
dangerous incident one should anticipate in future nuclear states occurred in early 1992 at the Ignalina nuclear
power plant in Lithuania, where a programmer reported
that he had found a virus in the computer that ran the
safety systems for the plant. Investigators later believed,
however, that he had placed the virus there himself in
order to receive a pay bonus for improving safety.[83] Finally, domestic political unrest can increase the risk of
nuclear weapons accidents by encouraging unsafe transportation, exercise, or testing operations. If warheads are
moved out of unstable regions in haste (as occurred in

the USSR in 1991) or if weapons tests are rushed to prevent rebellious military units from gaining access to the weapons (as occurred in Algeria in 1961[84]), safety is likely to be compromised. The most dramatic example of risky actions induced by domestic crises is Marshal Nie Rongzhen's decision to launch a test missile 800 kilometers across China, with a live nuclear warhead onboard, in October 1966 in the middle of the Cultural Revolution. Nie was apparently fully aware of the risks involved in such an unprecedented test, but believed that the nuclear weapons program needed a dramatic and public sign of success as part of his "strategy of siding with the radicals to fend off radical penetration of the program."[85]

In short, while there have been no catastrophic nuclear weapons accidents in the new nuclear states yet, there are good reasons to anticipate that the probabilities will be high over time. Any serious nuclear weapons accident will have tragic consequences for the local community; and if an accidental detonation, false warning, or unauthorized use of a weapon leads to "mistaken retaliation" and accidental war, the consequences would be even more catastrophic. As long as would-be nuclear states choose not to cross the final threshold of "weaponization" by actually deploying fully assembled nuclear weapons and launchers, these safety problems will largely remain dormant. Once these states begin to deploy arsenals, however, such organizational safety problems are likely to emerge rapidly. The current positive safety record is therefore likely to be only the lull before the storm.

CONCLUSIONS: BRINGING ORGANIZATIONS BACK IN

The nuclear optimists' view that the spread of nuclear weapons will produce stable deterrence is based on a rationalist assumption that the behavior of new nuclear states will reflect their interest in avoiding nuclear war. New nuclear powers will avoid preventive nuclear wars, develop survivable nuclear arsenals, and prevent nuclear weapons accidents because it is in their obvious national interests to do so. I have argued, in contrast, that the actual behavior of new proliferators will be strongly influenced by military organizations within those states and that the common biases, rigid routines, and parochial interests of these military organizations will lead to deterrence failures and accidental uses of nuclear weapons despite national interests to the contrary. The concepts behind this more pessimistic vision of proliferation are well-grounded in the rich theoretical and empirical literature on complex organizations. My theory makes less heroic assumptions about the rationality of states. It provides useful insights into U.S. nuclear history during the Cold War, and it points to the checks-and-balances system of civilian control as a critical factor in creating the requirements of nuclear deterrence during the long peace. Although the jury of history is still out on the consequences of further nuclear proliferation, and will be for some time, the emerging evidence from the nuclear-proliferating world unfortunately supports this more pessimistic view.

Bringing Organizations Back into International Relations Theory

By assuming that all nuclear states will behave quite rationally and will therefore take all the necessary steps to fulfill the requirements of deterrence, Waltz and other nuclear proliferation optimists have confused prescriptions of what rational states *should* do with predictions of what real states *will* do. This is an error that the classical American realists rarely committed: Hans Morgenthau and George Kennan believed that states should follow the logic of balance-of-power politics, but their whole enterprise was animated by a fear that the U.S. would fail to do so.[86] This is also an error that Waltz avoided in *Theory of International Politics*, where he noted that "the theory requires no assumptions of rationality . . . the theory says simply that if some do relatively well, others will emulate them or fall by the wayside."[87]

Adding this element of natural selection to a theory of international relations puts less of a burden on the assumption of rationality. My approach is consistent with this vision. Many nuclear states may well behave sensibly, but some will not and will then "fall by the wayside." Falling by the wayside, however, means using their nuclear weapons in this case and thus has very serious implications for the whole international system.

"Realist theory by itself can handle some, but not all the problems that concern us," Waltz correctly noted in 1986. "Just as market theory at times requires a theory of the firm, so international-political theory at times needs a theory of the state."[88] Understanding the consequences of nuclear proliferation is precisely one case in point. To predict the nuclear future, we need to utilize ideas, building upon the theory of the firm, about how and when common organizational behaviors can constrain rational reactions to the nuclear revolution.

If this analysis is correct, there is a great need for more research and writing at the organizational level of analysis in international relations. Many important questions remain unanswered, even concerning military organizations and proliferation. What is the eventual effect of nuclear weapons and other weapons of mass destruction on civil-military relations in new states that acquire such technologies? Can military organizations in the developing world learn vicariously from the experience of other professional militaries, or will they have to make their own successes and mistakes? What is the impact of organizational rigidities and interests within the state on the diffusion of international norms concerning the acquisition and use of highly destructive weapons? Theoretical and empirical research on such organizational-level issues will be critical to understanding international security in the post–Cold War world.[89]

Bringing Organizations into Counter-Proliferation Policy

What are the policy implications of my organizational-level approach to nuclear proliferation? First, and most obviously, this approach suggests that the United States is quite correct to maintain an active nuclear nonproliferation policy. A world with more nuclear-armed states may be our fate; it should not be our goal. It is highly unfortunate, in this regard, that a growing number of defense analysts in new nuclear nations read the arguments of the U.S. nuclear optimists, most prominently the writings of Kenneth Waltz, and now cite that literature to legitimize the development of nuclear arsenals in their nations.[90] It is fortunate, however, that U.S. government officials have not been convinced of the merits of the optimists' views, and there is little evidence that U.S. policy is going to move away from its strong opposition to the further spread of nuclear weapons.

Second, a more effective approach to nuclear proliferation would add a larger dose of intellectual persuasion to our current policy efforts, which are aimed primarily at restricting the supply of materials and providing security guarantees to potential nuclear states. There are ongoing debates—often in secret, sometimes in the open—about the wisdom of developing nuclear weapons in many of these countries. To influence such debates, nonproliferation advocates need to develop better understandings of the perceptions and interests of the domestic organizational actors involved. Decisionmakers in potential nuclear powers do not need to be told that proliferation is not in the *United States's* interests. They need to be convinced that it is not in *their* interest. Civilian leaders, military leaders, and wider publics alike in these states need to be reminded that the development of nuclear weapons will make their states targets for preventive attacks by their potential adversaries, will not easily lead to survivable arsenals, and will raise the specter of accidental or unauthorized uses of nuclear weapons. Just as importantly, they also need to be persuaded that nuclear proliferation may not be in their narrow self-interest as civilian leaders seeking for political power, as militaries seeking autonomy, and as citizens seeking safety.

Finally, an organizational approach offers a valuable, but pessimistic, perspective on efforts to manage proliferation if it occurs despite U.S. attempts to prevent it. At one level, an implication of an organizational perspective is that the United States should cooperate with new nuclear states—sharing knowledge of organizational structures, technology, and experience—to reduce the dangerous consequences of the spread of nuclear weapons. At a deeper level, however, the most disturbing lesson of this analysis is that, for organizational reasons, such cooperative efforts are not likely to succeed.

This is true with respect to all three of the requirements of deterrence. First, the most important step the United States could take to reduce the likelihood of military biases leading to preventive war in the new nuclear nations would be to encourage sustained civilian control of the military, with appropriate checks and balances, in those states. Such efforts are unlikely, however, to be completely effective. In some new nuclear states, strong military organizations are unlikely to give up their current positions of significant decisionmaking power and influence. In some other nuclear states, unpopular civilian regimes will not create competent, professional military organizations, since they might serve as a threat to the regime's power. In either case, appropriate civil-military relations are problematic. Efforts to improve civil-military relations are therefore likely to be most effective precisely where they are least needed.

Second, to enhance survivability of new nuclear forces, the United States could also consider cooperating with new nuclear states—sharing information on delivery-system technology, operational practices, and advanced warning systems—to help them create invulnerable forces.[91] This policy, however, is also unlikely to be widely implemented. Not only will U.S. policymakers fear that such cooperative efforts would signal that the United States is not really opposed to the further spread of nuclear weapons, but the leaders of new nuclear states, and especially the leaders of their military organizations, will also not want to discuss such sensitive issues in detail, fearing that it will expose their own nuclear vulnerabilities and organizational weaknesses to the United States.

Third, the large risk of nuclear accidents in these countries suggests that the United States may want to share information on such subjects as electronic locking devices, weapons-safety design improvements, and personnel reliability programs.[92] To the degree that the United States can share technology that only improves weapons safety and security, but does not enhance readiness to use the forces, such efforts would be helpful. A broad policy to make the weapons of new nuclear nations safer could be highly counterproductive, however, if it led them to believe that they could safely operate large nuclear arsenals on high states of alert.

Indeed, an organizational perspective on nuclear safety suggests that we need a paradigm shift in the way we think about managing proliferation. The United States should not try to make new nuclear nations become like the superpowers during the Cold War, with large arsenals ready to launch at a moment's notice for the sake of deterrence; instead, for the sake of safety, the United States and Russia should try to become more like some of the nascent nuclear states, maintaining very small nuclear capabilities, with weapons components separated and located apart from the delivery systems, and with civilian organizations controlling the warheads.

Finally, if my theories are right, the U.S. defense department should be telling new nuclear states, loudly and often, that there are inherent limits to nuclear weapons safety. If my theories are right, however, the U.S. defense department will not do this, because this would require it to acknowledge to others, and itself, how dangerous our own nuclear history has been. The important and difficult task of persuasion will therefore fall largely upon individuals outside the organizations that have managed U.S. nuclear weapons.

Chapter 3

WALTZ RESPONDS TO SAGAN

Kenneth N. Waltz

I. Introduction

"War is like love," the chaplain says in Bertolt Brecht's *Mother Courage*, "it always finds a way." For half a century, *nuclear* war has not found a way. The old saying, "accidents will happen," is translated as Murphy's Law holding that anything that can go wrong will go wrong. Enough has gone wrong, and Scott Sagan has recorded many of the nuclear accidents that have, or have nearly, taken place. Yet none of them has caused anybody to blow anybody else up. In a speech given to American scientists in 1960, C. P. Snow said this: "We know, with the certainty of statistical truth, that if enough of these weapons are made—by enough different states—some of them are going to blow up. Through accident, or folly, or madness—but the motives don't matter. What does matter is the nature of the statistical fact." In 1960, statistical fact told Snow that within "at the most, ten years some of these bombs are going off." Statistical fact now tells us that we are twenty-five years overdue. But the novelist and scientist overlooked the fact that there are no "statistical facts."[1]

Half a century of nuclear peace has to be explained since divergence from historical experience is dramatic.

Never in modern history, conventionally dated from 1648, have the great and major powers of the world enjoyed such a long period of peace. Scott Sagan emphasizes the problems and the conditions that conduce to pessimism. I emphasize the likely solutions and the conditions that conduce to optimism, bearing in mind that nothing in this world is ever certain.

II. Problems and Dangers

In section A, I consider a subject I neglected in Chapter 1: the possibility of terrorists bands gaining control of nuclear warheads. In sections B through E, I consider problems that supposedly grow as nuclear weapons spread slowly from country to country. In doing so, I reflect on concerns Scott Sagan expresses in Chapter 2.

A. Terror

With the devolution of nuclear weapons to three of the parts of the former Soviet Union, with shaky control of nuclear weapons materials in Russia, with the revelation in 1994 that the United States had lost track of some of its nuclear materials, with increased numbers of countries able and perhaps willing to sell components needed to develop nuclear capability to countries that lack them, and with a flourishing market in systems for the delivery of weapons, fear has grown that terrorists may obtain nuclear explosives and means of placing them on targets they choose. The worry is real, especially if terrorists are eager to have nuclear explosives and are backed by a state bent on disrupting international society.

Terrorists have done a good bit of damage by using conventional weapons and have sometimes got their way by threatening to use them. By their lights, might terrorists not do better still by threatening to explode nuclear weapons on cities of countries they may wish to bend to their bidding?

If we believe that terrorists could, if they wished to, wield nuclear weapons to threaten or damage their chosen enemies, then the important question becomes: Why would they want to? To answer this question, we have to ask further what terrorists are trying to do and what means best suit their ends.

Terrorists do not play their deadly games to win in the near term. Their horizons are distant. Instead they try to offer a voice to the unheard, to give a glimmer of hope to the forlorn, to force established societies to recognize alienated others previously unseen, and ultimately to transcend given societies and found their own.

Terrorists live precarious lives. Nobody trusts them, not even those who finance, train, and hide them. If apprehended, they cannot count on the help of others. They have learned how to use conventional weapons to some effect. Nuclear weapons would thrust them into a world fraught with new dangers.

Terrorists work in small groups. Secrecy is safety, yet to obtain and maintain nuclear weapons would require enlarging the terrorist band through multiplication of suppliers, transporters, technicians, and guardians. Inspiring devotion, instilling discipline, and ensuring secrecy become harder tasks to accomplish as numbers grow. Moreover, as the demands of terrorists increase, compliance with their demands becomes harder to secure. If, for example, terrorists had told Israel to abandon the occupied territories or suffer the nuclear destruction of Tel Aviv, Israel's compliance would have required that a lengthy and difficult political process be carried through. However they may be armed, terrorists are not capable of maintaining pressure while lengthy efforts toward compliance are made.

One more point should be made before concluding this section. If terrorists should unexpectedly decide to

abandon tactics of disruption and harassment in favor of
dealing in threats of wholesale death and destruction, instruments other than nuclear weapons are more easily
available. Poisons are easier to get and use than nuclear
weapons, and poisoning a city's water supply is more
easily done than blowing the city up.

Fear of nuclear terror arises from the assumption
that if terrorists *can* get nuclear weapons they *will* get
them, and that then all hell will break lose. This is comparable to assuming that if weak states get nuclear
weapons, they will use them for aggression. Both assumptions are false. Would the courses of action we fear,
if followed, promise more gains than losses or more
pains than profits? The answers are obvious. Terrorists
have some hope of reaching their long-term goals
through patient pressure and constant harassment. They
cannot hope to do so by issuing unsustainable threats to
wreck great destruction, threats they would not want to
execute anyway.

B. Accidents

The more nuclear weapons there are, and the larger the
number of countries that have them, the likelier it is that
some will go off. That is C. P. Snow's reasoning, and it is
the common wisdom. The United States has been lax in
devising safety measures and has often found them difficult to apply. The American navy, unlike the Soviet
navy, refused to use PALS (permissive action links), a
system designed to prevent unauthorized firings. A former Minuteman missile launcher (Bruce Blair) and an
M.I.T. physicist (Henry Kendall), wonder why even now
we keep our ICBMs (intercontinental ballistic missiles) on
hair-trigger alert.[2] The main hazards, they plausibly argue, are unauthorized firings and firings that result from
false warning. Keeping large numbers of strategic missiles ready to go in thirty minutes increases the danger.

Hair-trigger forces are no longer needed, if they ever were, yet we continue to have them.[3]

When countries venture into the nuclear game, smallness of numbers works strongly against their accidentally firing nuclear weapons. Small countries fret about the damage they may suffer through retaliation if one or several of their warheads go astray. They guard them with almost paranoiac zeal. Because countries, especially poor ones, can build sizable forces only over long periods of time, they have time to learn how to care for them.

Sagan is leery of the cognitive abilities of political leaders. Aren't we all? Yet some do better than others. Survival is an interesting test of learning ability. We continually worry about the leaders of "rogue" states —the likes of Qaddafi, Saddam, and Kim Il Sung. Yet they survived for many years, despite great internal and external dangers. Their cognitive skills, in the crabbed language of social scientists, are more impressive than those of, say, Jimmy Carter or George Bush. Given all of the advantages of presidential incumbency, Carter and Bush managed to stay in office for only four years. American politics is gentle compared to the politics of the countries that have recently joined, or are likely to join, the nuclear club. Are hardy political survivors in the Third World likely to run the greatest of all risks by drawing the wrath of the world down on them by accidentally or in anger exploding nuclear weapons they may have?

At least some of the rulers of new and prospective nuclear states are thought to be ruthless, reckless, and war-prone. Ruthless, yes; war-prone, seldom; reckless, hardly. They do not, as many seem to believe, have fixed images of the world and unbending aims within it. Instead they have to adjust constantly to a shifting configuration of forces around them. Our images of leaders of Third World states vary remarkably little, yet their agility is remarkable.

The preceding points are important and often overlooked. Whatever the identity of rulers, and whatever
the characteristics of their states, the national behaviors
they produce are strongly conditioned by the world outside. With conventional weapons, a status-quo country
must ask itself how much power it must harness to its
policy in order to dissuade an aggressive state from
striking. Countries willing to run high risks are hard to
dissuade. The characteristics of governments and the
temperaments of leaders have to be carefully weighed.
With nuclear weapons, any state will be deterred by another state's second-strike forces. One need not be preoc-
cupied with the qualities of the state that is to be deterred or scrutinize its leaders.

America has long associated democracy with peace
and authoritarianism with war, overlooking that weak
authoritarian states often avoid war for fear of upsetting
the balance of internal and external forces on which their
power depends. Neither Italy nor Germany was able to
persuade Franco's Spain to enter World War II. External
pressures affect state behavior with a force that varies
with conditions. Of all of the possible external forces,
what could affect state behavior more strongly than nuclear weapons? Who cares about the "cognitive" abilities
of leaders when nobody but an idiot can fail to comprehend their destructive force? What more is there to
learn? How can leaders miscalculate? For a country to
strike first without certainty of success, all of those who
control a nation's nuclear weapons would have to go
mad at the same time. Nuclear reality transcends political rhetoric. Did our own big words, or the Soviet Union's prattling about nuclear war-fighting, ever mean
anything? Political, military, and academic hard-liners
imagined conditions under which we would or should be
willing to use nuclear weapons. None was of relevance.
Nuclear weapons dominate strategy. Nothing can be
done with them other than to use them for deterrence.

The United States and the Soviet Union were both reluctant to accept the fact of deterrence. Weaker states find it easier to substitute deterrence for war-fighting, precisely because they are weak.

C. Civilian Control

The United States has a long tradition of civilian control of the military. Most, if not all, of the recent and prospective nuclear states lack both the tradition and the practice of civilian control. This worries Sagan more than it does me. The following three considerations reduce or eliminate the worries.

First, civilian control in the United States is not as sure as many believe it to be. A few examples illustrate the point. President Harry S. Truman ordered that the defense budget for fiscal year 1950 not exceed $15 billion, of which $600 million was for stockpiling materials that might be needed in a prolonged war. Secretary of Defense James Forrestal appointed a board headed by retired General McNarney. The board came up with a military plan estimated to cost $23.6 billion. Forrestal thereupon ordered the Joint Chiefs of Staff to come up with a plan that he might be able to sell to the president, a plan that would cost about $17.5 billion. The Joint Chiefs refused, and Forrestal lacked the authority to bring them to heel.[4] With effective civilian control, military officers would have had to come up with a strategy within the budgetary limits set by the executive branch. They refused to do so.

President Dwight D. Eisenhower became more and more concerned in the later years of his presidency with the military's plans to fire hundreds or thousands of warheads at the Soviet Union if the occasion for retaliation should arise. He worried that force would be used in ways that would create an ungovernable postwar world.[5] Even with all of his military prestige, Eisenhower found control of the military difficult, if not impossible, to achieve.[6]

Early in President John F. Kennedy's presidency, Secretary of Defense McNamara, Jerome Wiesner, and a few others asked themselves how many ICBMs we needed. They first came up with the number two hundred. Concerns about misfirings and force vulnerability led them to double the number. McNamara nevertheless asked Congress to authorize one thousand ICBMs, not four hundred. He did so for two main reasons. He and his advisors feared that the air force would weigh in with a request for three thousand. At the time counterforce, aiming weapons at weapons, versus countervalue, aiming weapons at cities, was much debated. McNamara at first favored the former.[7] About one hundred Soviet cities were thought to be worth striking, in my view an absurdly high number. The air force, however, identified counterforce targets in the Soviet Union numbering in the thousands. Rather than ask Congress for the number he thought to be appropriate, McNamara asked for one thousand. Why? He thought that he could defend that number in congressional committee hearings against whatever the air force claimed that it needed. The second reason for McNamara's choosing the higher number is that President Kennedy wanted to conclude a test ban treaty with the Soviet Union. To get a treaty through the Senate would require the support, or at least the acquiescence, of the Joint Chiefs. As it is between states, so it is between civilian and military leaders—if allies are needed one has to do some things to please them.

These examples, among many I can think of, show that civilian control is not something that simply exists by constitutional and other laws. It has to be maintained through persistent and hard work, lest civilian control of the military give way to military control of the military. In the Kennedy and Johnson administrations, the Department of Defense firmly controlled the military until it became bogged down in trying to run the war in Vietnam. Prior to the Eisenhower administration's "New Look" defense policy, each of the services received about one-third of the defense budget. The "New Look" sharply skewed the distribution of dollars in favor of the air force: almost 50 percent of the budget for it, approximately 30 percent for the navy, and just over 20 percent for the army. One can tell when civilians are exercising control by the yelps of protest from military officers, sometimes followed by their resignations.[8] Under President Richard M. Nixon and Defense Secretary Melvin Laird, the budgetary division among the services quickly reverted to one-third, one-third, one-third, reflecting Laird's boast that under him the United States would have a budget made by the military. Later, when he was secretary of Defense, Caspar Weinberger also let the services write their own tickets; a huge waste of dollars, with little gain in strength, was the country's reward.

Civilian control is won and maintained only by constant and politically costly effort. Some states accept military control of the military, but this simply puts them in the same position that the United States often finds itself in.

Second, Sagan believes that civilian control of the military makes the world safer, and military control of the military makes the world more dangerous. I believe that either way the world is at peril. Historically, one notices that civilian leaders are sometimes, indeed fairly often, more reckless than military officers. In Chapter 1, I gave the Crimean War as an example. Military officers who saw the war coming called it an "impossible war." As the historian Alfred Vagts wrote, "the nonmilitary were warlike and the military were not."[9] Britain and France lacked the troops that would enable them to invade the Russian heartland. Luckily for them, the czar rejected the strategy that General Kutuzov had used to defeat Napoleon: retreat, draw the enemy into Russia's vast territory, and when supply lines lengthened and troops wearied, turn upon them and drive them from the land. Because the czar sat shakily on his throne, he feared that retreat would be seen as defeat and he would be deposed. For political rather than military reasons, he sent his troops to the Crimea where British and French troops, disembarking at Black Sea ports, could meet them.

Like civilian leaders, military officers have interests. The belief is widespread that, when military responses to crises are infeasible, military officers favor the use of force. The belief has often proved false. The common quality of military advice is caution, as a number of examples show. In the Moroccan crises of 1905 and 1911, military ministers and officers in France and Russia warned strongly against using force. American military leaders prior to World War II urged softer diplomacy and re-duced economic pressure, fearing that stronger policies would goad Japan to a war they did not want at that time. Generals George Marshall and Omar Bradley op-posed General Douglas MacArthur's policy of carrying the war in Korea across the Yalu River and into Man-churia. The Pentagon in 1958 opposed sending marines to Lebanon, a policy the State Department favored. American military leaders in 1983 opposed sending troops to Grenada quickly, perhaps because they wanted first to find it on the map, and in July of 1994, Pentagon officials strongly opposed invading Haiti.[10] Now, even worse, we have military control, or heavy influence, over civil government. General Colin Powell oversaw the writing of Defense Secretary Caspar Weinberger's 1984 speech setting forth six criteria to be met before using American forces abroad. The so-called Weinberger Doc-trine proposed that we fight only wars that can be quickly and sweetly won. In doing so, he identified the military's interest with the national interest. Publicly, Powell offered his own opinions on foreign policy "in contravention," as military historian Richard H. Kohn put it, "to the tradition of American civil-military relations since the beginning of the republic." Kohn concludes, after giving a number of examples, that for some years now we have seen "the erosion of civilian control of the military."[11]

What is the point? Simply this: If the weakness or absence of civilian control of the military has not led America to use its plentiful nuclear weapons, we hardly have reason to think that new nuclear countries will misuse theirs because of an absence of civilian control.

Yet Sagan is right to emphasize that military officers have at times advocated preventive wars and preemptive strikes, although one must add that so have civilians. Ultimately, the military's concern is for national security. If civilian and military leaders think that their state is strong now but that an adversary may one day surpass it, then national leaders thump for preventive war. At times military officers have urged preventive war, and political leaders have opposed it. Such cases occur not because soldiers or civilians lust for blood, but because they worry about their nation's security. Most of Sagan's examples of America's preventive-war spirit come from the early Cold War years. We once had a monopoly of nuclear weapons followed by a wide superiority. Numerical superiority did not mean much, if anything, but unsurprisingly, military *and* civilian leaders thought it did. The idea of using a temporary military edge for one's advantage finds many precedents. We should remember, however, that preventive wars have been advocated many more times than they have been fought.

The situation that invites preventive-war thinking is this: State A believes itself to be initially in a superior position and fears that it may one day be surpassed by State B [see Figure 1]. The American–Soviet picture is shown in Figure 2. Americans should easily understand the mentality that prompts preventive-war thinking. We have fought enough of them. President Bush's war against Panama was a preventive one. Nobody thought that Panama posed either a near-term or a long-term threat to the United States. We were not fighting for an American vital interest. One cannot even say what threats to our national security we were trying to prevent. More recently, we fought another preventive war, this one against Iraq. We could easily have deterred Iraq from invading any more countries, and the world did not need Iraq's or Kuwait's oil. Iraq and Kuwait together produced about 7 percent of the world's oil supply. What we feared was that Saddam would control the large oil *reserves* of Iraq and Kuwait combined, about 20 percent of the world's total. We feared how Saddam might use oil power not at the moment but in the future. Was it plausible to say that we needed to fight a country of fewer than 19 million people in order to control the future?

To say that a war should be fought preventively requires betting that the unknowable future will be a better one if an unnecessary war is fought now instead of waiting to see if it one day becomes necessary. "Unnecessary" means that the present threat to one's interest

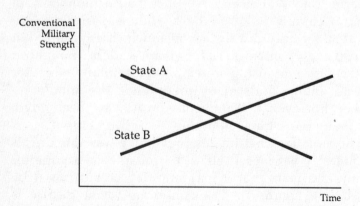

FIGURE 1

is not pressing. The reasoning goes this way: We do not need to fight now, but fighting now will be easy, and we'll win. Fighting later will be hard, and we may lose. To make a case for preventive war, one has to know that the balance of effective forces is roughly as the first figure shows, that the future development of forces is as depicted, and that in the end one side will fight the other. In a conventional world, the first two suppositions are suspect; in any world, the third one is as well. The second figure shows a different relation between two countries: one initially with some, or perhaps many, nuclear weapons; the other with none. If A (in this case, the United States) chooses to forego striking to prevent B (the Soviet Union) from making *any* nuclear weapons, then a preemptive strike by A against B becomes risky at an early stage of the competition.

Why preventive wars are not fought is an easily answered question. Why nuclear states have shrunk from striking to prevent other states from gaining nuclear capability in the first place may seem more puzzling. Would we and the world be better off if we had erased

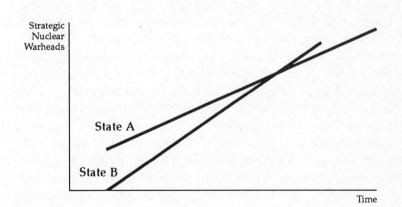

FIGURE 2

the Soviet Union earlier, or if we had destroyed its nuclear facilities and its bombs later? Would we and the world be better off now if the United States or the Soviet Union had destroyed China's budding nuclear capability in the early 1960s? One may even believe that if Israel had failed to destroy Iraq's nuclear facilities in 1981, the two countries would have soon settled into a stable, if unfriendly, relation of mutual deterrence, as others did before them.

To think that civilian leaders understand the problematic qualities of preventive-war arguments, and that military leaders do not, is wrong. Some do; some do not. President Bush did not. General Norman Schwarzkopf and I made the mistake of believing Bush when he said on August 7, 1990, that our response to Iraq's invasion of Kuwait would be defensive. Schwarzkopf defined his mission in accordance with what the president said: "Our mission is to deter attack, and if an attack comes, we are to defend." But on that fateful day, November 8, 1990, two days after congressional elections, Bush announced a decision that had been made earlier: namely, to increase our deployment from a force of about 200,000 to a force of more than 500,000. He went from a force large enough to dissuade Saddam from further attacks to a force large enough to take the offensive. Once we moved to a force of more than half a million, which, with the forces of allies, made a total of more than 700,000 troops, it became hard to wait. Bush and Secretary of Defense Richard Cheney led the way toward fighting a preventive war. Secretary of State James Baker followed with reluctance. The most reluctant of all—not surprisingly—were army and marine generals. Admirals and air force generals are often more willing to go because they believe they can win by dropping bombs and shooting weapons at distant targets. In late January of 1991, General Schwarzkopf said that "if the alternative to dying is sitting out in the sun for another summer, then that's not

a bad alternative." Notice what a strong statement that
was. He was not saying that we should wait a few more
months but that we should be willing to sit in the desert
sun for another summer. He was saying as clearly as he
could, without flatly contradicting the president, that we
did not need to go to war at all. We could have sat there,
while giving sanctions time to work. If we had stuck
with a much smaller force, we could have afforded to
wait. Instead, our civilian leaders chose to fight.[12]

Third, Sagan believes that military leaders are more
reckless and war-prone than civilian leaders are. I find
this hard to believe. In the late 1930s, German generals
knew that the balance of forces favored the British and
French in aircraft, tanks, artillery, and manpower.[13] Their
troops could have poured through the thin Siegfried Line
when Germany took Austria or when it took the Sudetenland or when it took the rest of Czechoslovakia or
when it invaded Poland. German generals understood
this, and some of them stood against Hitler's policy.
Hitler may have understood this too, but he acted on
political insight rather than on military calculation,
believing that France and Britain would not move. He
was right, but only in the short run. Military organizations tend toward caution; civilian leaders sometimes do
not.

Big and long wars work profound economic, social,
political, and even cultural changes in the countries that
fight them. The biggest change of all takes place in military organizations. World War II is a sufficient example.
Regular military officers in the United States spent four
years at West Point or Annapolis before earning com-
missions. Draftees, kids like me with no military back-
ground, could do four months of basic and advanced
training, go to officer-candidate school for another four
months, and become commissioned officers. World War
II affected America's military services even more pro-
foundly than it affected society at large.

The traditionalism of soldiers and sailors is rein-
forced by the fact that they are not professionals. Instead, they are members of establishments. The difference is this: Professionals can hang their shingles any-
where. They can set their legal or medical practices up,
work for any law firm or hospital, teach in any college or
university that will have them. In contrast, members of
an establishment have one legitimate employer, in this
case, the military services. They may become free booters
or seek non-military employment, but if they want to
pursue the trade they trained for, they have to stick with
the military organizations that prepared them for service.
Members of an establishment develop unusually strong
commitments to their organizations. This reinforces their
conservatism.

Generals and admirals do not like to fight wars under unfamiliar conditions. The offensive use of nuclear
weapons exponentially increases the uncertainties that
abound on conventional battlefields. Nobody knows
what a nuclear battlefield would look like, and nobody
knows what would happen after a few nuclear shots
were fired. *Uncertainty* about the course that a nuclear
war might follow, along with *certainty* that destruction
could be immense, strongly inhibits the use of nuclear
weapons.

D. Second-Strike Forces

Can weak and poor states manage to deploy second-strike
forces? The answer is "yes," quite easily. This answer con-
tradicts Sagan's, and many others', belief that second-
strike forces are difficult to build and deploy. Decades of
American military worries feed this view. But as Bernard
Brodie put it, if a "small nation could threaten the Soviet
Union with only a single thermonuclear bomb, which,
however, it could and would certainly deliver on Moscow," the Soviet Union would be deterred.[14] I would

change that sentence by substituting "might" for "would" and by adding that the threat of a fission bomb or two would also do the trick. We now know that Britain, thinking as we did that the Soviet Union was hard to deter, pretended to have H-bombs when it had none.[15] Sagan believes that the American air force and navy had to be goaded into developing second-strike forces. He cites the Killian Report of 1955, written by civilians, as providing the push that caused the military to become concerned with the survivability of strategic weapons. In one sense, he is right. Our military services were more interested in their traditional missions and weapons than they were in nuclear deterrence. The navy's initial response to the Polaris program was to say that it was a national program, not a naval one. (Eisenhower wondered what the difference might be.) An unconventional naval officer, Hyman Rickover, drove the program through ahead of time and on budget. For this, the navy never forgave him. Congress had to add his name to the lists of officers to be promoted because the navy would not do so. Military organizations are renowned for their resistance to innovation.

Yet once a country has a small number of deliverable warheads of uncertain location, it has a second-strike force. Belatedly, some Americans and Russians realized this.[16] Former secretary Robert S. McNamara wrote in 1985 that the United States and the Soviet Union could get along with 2,000 warheads instead of the 50,000 they may then have had.[17] Talking at the University of California, Berkeley, in the spring of 1992, he dropped the number the United States might need to sixty. Herbert York, speaking at the Lawrence Livermore National Laboratory, which he once directed, guessed that one hundred strategic warheads would be about the right number for us.[18] It does not take much to deter.

The ease of deterrence raises the question of whether it was the Killian Report that pushed the military services to develop second-strike forces or whether we already had them. With an estimated 1,500 strategic warheads in our hands and 150 to 700 in the Soviet Union's hands, both had invulnerable forces. Who would dare to strike forces of that size when neither the United States nor the Soviet Union could be sure of destroying or disabling all of them? With nuclear weapons, if any part of a force is invulnerable, all of the force is invulnerable. Who will risk retaliation by the portion of a force that survives one's strike?[19] During the Cuban missile crisis, for example, the Tactical Air Command would promise only that it could destroy 90 percent of the missiles the Soviet Union had placed in Cuba. Retaliation by the remaining 10 percent was unacceptable to us. This was at the time when we thought the Soviet missiles in Cuba were backed up by only about seventy strategic warheads.[20]

Numbers are not very important. To have second-strike forces, states do not need large numbers of weapons. Small numbers do quite nicely. About one-half of the South Korean population centers on Seoul. North Korea can deter South Korea and the United States from invading if it can lead the South to believe that it has a few well-hidden and deliverable weapons. The requirements of second-strike deterrence have been widely and wildly exaggerated.

E. Uncertainty

Sagan thinks I put too much weight on the beneficial effects of uncertainty. Yet the effectiveness of nuclear deterrence rests on uncertainty. Because no one can be sure that a major conventional attack on a nuclear country's vital interests will not escalate to the nuclear level, it is deterred. Uncertainty about controlling escalation is at the heart of deterrence. If the United States had thought that Iraq might have had a few bombs, it would have had to manage the Iraq-Kuwait crisis differently, say by employing only an embargo. Invasion *might* have prompted Iraq to dump a couple of warheads on Haifa and Tel Aviv. We would not have wanted to run the risk, and Israel surely would not have complained about our unwillingness to use force in a headlong attack. A big reason for America's resistance to the spread of nuclear weapons is that if weak countries have some they will cramp our style. Militarily punishing small countries for behavior we dislike would become much more perilous.

Deterrence is also a considerable guarantee against accidents, since it causes countries to take good care of their weapons, and against anonymous use, since those firing the weapons can neither know that they will be undetected nor what form of punishment detection might bring. In life, uncertainties abound. In a conventional world, they more easily lead to war because less is at stake. Even so, it is difficult to think of wars that have started by accident even before nuclear weapons were invented. It is hard to believe that nuclear war may begin accidentally, when less frightening conventional wars have rarely done so.[21]

Fear of accidents works against their occurring. Again this is illustrated by the Cuban Missile Crisis. Accidents happened during the crisis, and unplanned events took place. An American U-2 strayed over Siberia, and one flew over Cuba. The American navy continued to play games at sea, such games as trying to force Soviet submarines to surface. In a crisis, presidents and party chairmen wanted to control all relevant actions, while knowing they could not do so. Fear of losing control propelled Kennedy and Khrushchev to end the crisis quickly. In a conventional world, uncertainty may tempt a country to join battle. In a nuclear world, uncertainty has the opposite effect. What is not surely controllable is too dangerous to bear.

III. CONCLUSION

In the conclusion I make four points. They reinforce what I have said earlier and add a little to it.

First, in a lead editorial, the *New York Times* urged that something be done to roll "back the nuclear arms race on the subcontinent." That "will require," the editorial added, "India and Pakistan to address their insecurity by building mutual confidence and reducing the risk of war."[22] These are exactly the effects that the mutual possession of nuclear weapons produce, as some Indians and Pakistanis have come to realize. To cite a variation on a common theme, in an article in the *New York Times* by Steven Erlanger, we read this: "If Kiev keeps its missiles, anxiety will increase." One wonders whose anxiety will increase, and why. Ukraine's ambassador to Washington made more sense when he said that Ukraine's weapons are "a powerful means of deterrence."[23]

Second, we can play King Canute if we wish to, but like him, we will be unable to hold the (nuclear) tides at bay. Nuclear weapons have spread slowly; conventional weapons have proliferated, and their destructiveness has grown alarmingly. Nuclear weapons are relatively cheap, and they work against the outbreak of major wars. For some countries, the alternative to nuclear weapons is to run ever-more expensive conventional arms races, with increased risk of fighting highly destructive wars.

Third, Sagan and others use the term "deterrence theory" or even "rational deterrence theory." Deterrence is not a theory. Instead, deterrent policies derive from structural theory, which emphasizes that the units of an international-political system must tend to their own security as best they can. The means available for doing so shape the policies of states and, when nuclear weapons become available, lead them in fact to take deterrent stances even though they may still talk about the need to be able to defend and to fight for their nations' security.[24] In applying theories, one considers salient conditions in the world, and nothing is more salient than nuclear weapons. Moreover, deterrence does not rest on rationality, whatever that term might mean. By a simple definition, one is rational if one is able to reason. A little reasoning leads to the conclusions that to fight nuclear wars is all but impossible and that to launch an offensive that might prompt nuclear retaliation is obvious folly. To reach those conclusions, complicated calculations are not required, only a little common sense.

Fourth, new nuclear countries may, as Sagan says, lack safety devices for their weapons and may not have developed bureaucratic routines for controlling them. The smaller a force is, however, the more easily it can be guarded. States with large arsenals and faulty bureaucratic routines may accidentally fire warheads in large numbers. States with small arsenals cannot do so. Blair and Kendall estimated that a Soviet attack accidentally launched against us might have resulted in as many as three hundred warheads falling on the United States. In response, as many as five hundred of our warheads might then have been launched against the Soviet Union.[25] A policy of launch on warning makes no sense. If a country is struck, retaliation at leisure, and calibration of one's response in an attempt to bring de-escalation, is called for. Only big nuclear powers can implement the frightening practices we follow. Little ones cannot because they don't have the stuff.

As ever in international politics, the biggest dangers come from the biggest powers; the smallest from the smallest. We should be more fearful of old nuclear countries and less fearful of recent and prospective ones. Efforts should concentrate more on making large arsenals safe and less on keeping weak states from obtaining the small number of warheads they may understandably believe they need for security.

Chapter 4

SAGAN RESPONDS TO WALTZ

Scott D. Sagan

There are two basic kinds of errors that one can make in assessing nations other than one's own. The first error is rooted in ethnocentrism. This is a common mistake Americans make when looking at others: we too often assume that other nations are less competent, less intelligent, and less rational than the United States. Kenneth Waltz has performed an important service in this regard: his analysis of nuclear proliferation is a valuable corrective against such ethnocentrism and the blind spots it can create among both scholars and government officials. He is absolutely correct, in my view, to criticize a number of proliferation pessimists who argue, in effect, that the United States has been perfect in handling nuclear weapons (but others will not be), that the United States can control these awesome weapons forever (but no one else can), or that the United States has utterly unproblematic civil-military relations (but no one else does). Waltz's analysis should serve as a constant reminder of how dangerous it is in international affairs to assume, to put it crudely, that the United States is smart, but that other nuclear states are or will be stupid.

The second basic error, however, is the opposite: to assume that others are better than we are. This is, I believe, the central problem with Kenneth Waltz's arguments about the consequences of proliferation. He now appears to accept many of the arguments made by scholars who have studied the operational accidents and near-accidents, conflicts in civil-military relations, and other organizational problems experienced by the United States during the Cold War. Yet he maintains that other states will do better, will be smarter, will learn more quickly, will, in short, avoid the kinds of errors that we have suffered in the past. I believe, in contrast, that there are both strong theoretical reasons and emerging empirical evidence to expect that new states will not avoid such problems. New nuclear powers may not make exactly the same mistakes as their predecessors; but they are likely to make their own serious errors, and some will be deadly.

THE ROOTS OF THE DISAGREEMENT

What lies at the heart of our disagreement? Let me start by strongly emphasizing what we do *not* disagree about. First, we do not disagree about the awesome destructive power of nuclear weapons. These weapons are horrendous. They dwarf conventional and even chemical weapons in their destructive potential. A single nuclear weapon can virtually destroy a modern city, an unprecedented level of destruction packed into a single bomb. Second, we do not, for the most part, disagree on the normative question of how states *should* behave in response to the nuclear revolution. Nuclear weapons states *should* be exceedingly cautious; they *should* place a high priority on nuclear weapons safety; they *should* build secure second-strike retaliatory forces for the sake of stable deterrence.[1]

What we disagree about is in some ways more fundamental. Waltz and I hold very different views about how best to explain and predict the behavior of states.

While we may agree about how nuclear states should behave in an *ideal* world (if any nuclear world can be called ideal), we strongly disagree about how nuclear states actually do behave in the *real* world. Our different visions of international politics lead us to develop both very different interpretations of our nuclear past and very different predictions of the nuclear future.

Waltz's optimism is fueled by a strong belief that the constraints of the international system, and the potential costs of any nuclear war, will produce similar, and essentially rational, decisions in all states. As he puts it, "Whatever the identity of rulers, and whatever the characteristics of their states, the national behaviors they produce are strongly conditioned by the world outside" (Ch. 3, p. 98). This assumption, that states will recognize and act on their "objective" interests as determined by external forces, undergirds his entire argument. In contrast, my pessimism is fueled by the belief that military and other government organizations play a very important intervening role between the interests of statesmen and the behavior of states. The information these organizations pass on, the plans and routines they develop, and the biases they hold, continually shape the actions of states in very important ways.

Waltz stresses the unprecedented power of nuclear weapons and argues that "nobody but an idiot can fail to comprehend their destructive force[.] What more is there to learn?" (Ch. 3, p.98). Unfortunately, there is a lot more to learn. States have to learn how to avoid accidents, how to build survivable forces, how to control their militaries, and how to limit escalation. All political leaders may well desire such reasonable things. Yet, between the desire and the deed lies the shadow of organizations. The difficult tasks of proper organizational design and management are not automatically achieved simply because senior statesmen understand the effects of nuclear weapons. And they certainly are not guaranteed to exist in every state that develops these horribly destructive weapons.

In this response, I will first discuss these organizational problems with respect to all three difficulties in deterrence—accidents, civilian control and preventive war, and second-strike capabilities—which are analyzed in my chapter and are disputed by Waltz in his spirited response. I will then comment on a related, and critical, issue in this debate: if nuclear weapons are used by accident or design, what are the risks of escalation? In the conclusions, I will present some ideas about future policy for nonproliferation and some final observations about international relations theory.

Accidents: Are They Likely?

Before the 1979 Three Mile Island accident, there was a widespread view among many specialists and much of the public that the risk of a reactor catastrophe was extremely low and that nuclear power had been rendered safe.[2] Before the 1985 space shuttle *Challenger* accident, NASA's confidence about space launch safety was so high that teachers and politicians were being permitted to join shuttle crews.[3] Throughout most of the Cold War, there was, I believe, a similar, significant underestimation of the risks of nuclear weapons accidents and even accidental nuclear war. Part of the reason for this underestimation was because we lacked adequate theories about the underlying political and organizational causes of accidents with hazardous technologies: only after Three Mile Island, Bhopal, and Chernobyl did social scientists enter the field in a significant way.[4] The other reason for this major underestimation, however, was more political in nature: there were strong reasons for the organizations that "control" nuclear weapons to insist that their safety record was unblemished. Even after serious accidents, such as when a nuclear bomber crashed in Greenland in 1968 or a nuclear missile blew up in Arkansas in 1980, the public was told that there were no serious risks involved. Don't worry, be happy was the message.

We now know better. Indeed, the history of the U.S. experience with nuclear weapons is being reevaluated in light of the number of nuclear accidents and near-accidents, false warning incidents, and other organizational snafus uncovered by scholars such as Bruce Blair, Paul Bracken, Peter Feaver, and myself.[5] Given this emerging evidence, even a hard-core neorealist like Waltz does not ignore the evidence that everything has not been perfectly safe inside the U.S. nuclear arsenal. He is certainly right to conclude now that, despite improvements made at the end of the Cold War, serious safety and security problems remain in the existing nuclear arsenals in the 1990s. Trident warheads for U.S. submarines continue to lack insensitive high explosives.[6] The U.S. and Russian decisions to suspend nuclear testing reduces certainty about safety in older warheads.[7] A post–Cold War loss of discipline and morale appears to be producing dangerous sabotage incidents and sloppy handling of weapons in the U.S. weapons production complex, and cases of nuclear theft in Russia.[8] Waltz is also correct, in my view, to argue that the United States maintains larger numbers of weapons at much higher states of readiness than are necessary in the post–Cold War world. Instead of concluding, however, that the fact that the richest and strongest nuclear power has had serious problems maintaining nuclear safety suggests that others will also suffer accidents, Waltz concludes the opposite. New members of the nuclear club will have fewer safety problems than the experienced ones. Why?

Waltz outlines three arguments for why new states will not have accidents: the small size of their arsenals, their fear of retaliation, and the possibility of learning over time. Each of these points is highly debatable. Let me take them in turn.

First, Waltz argues that the small size of the nuclear arsenals in new nuclear states makes accidents less likely. It may be true that the smaller the number of weapons, the less likely an accident, other things being equal. Unfortunately, in real life, other things are rarely equal. What produces the likelihood of accidents is not just the size of an arsenal, but rather the technical characteristics of the weapons themselves and the organizational characteristics of the arsenal. On the technical side, we should be worried about whether new nuclear states' weapons will be designed in a safe manner. The reports that the design of the Iraqi nuclear bomb was so flawed that it "could go off if a rifle bullet hit it" certainly are not comforting.[9] Similarly, when South African weapons engineers examined their first nuclear device, secretly constructed in the late 1970s, they considered it to be based on "an unqualified design that could not meet the rigid safety, security, and reliability specifications then under development."[10] Moreover, similar technical design problems could emerge and produce serious accidents with nuclear delivery systems and false warnings of attack from command-and-control and warning systems in new nuclear states. On the organizational side, the key issue concerns not the size, but the structure of any new state's arsenal. Is it complex and tightly-coupled? Here one needs to assess the command and control systems, the warning systems, and the launch doctrines of new nuclear states. States that develop complex arsenals and command systems, and operate their weapons on high-alert levels in order to permit rapid launches, will be more accident-prone than states that do not adopt such force structures.

Second, Waltz argues that new nuclear states will greatly fear retaliation, and will therefore make sure that their weapons are not used by accident or in an unauthorized manner. This is likely to be a leader's desire, but will it be the state's behavior? It is difficult to know, because strong contradictory pressures would exist in most new nuclear powers. On the one hand, strong incentives would certainly exist to keep such forces under very tight, centralized control, an argument that strongly cuts against the widespread fear that new nuclear states will try to sneak weapons into an adversary's territory in peacetime.[11] (A Third World leader, who has just spent a large portion of his or her GNP to build a small arsenal, might be very reluctant to then agree to deploy the weapons covertly in a foreign country where they might be found and destroyed by enemy police or security forces.) On the other hand, strong incentives would also exist to loosen such control in order to increase the likelihood that forces could retaliate after a first strike.[12]

Small arsenal size can have the opposite effect than what Waltz predicts. Fearing that an attack might destroy its forces, a small nuclear power will likely feel greater incentives to use increased missile alerts or unsafe aircraft operations (such as airborne alert), which inherently raise risks of accidents. Moreover, fearing a "decapitation" attack on its central leadership bunkers (as the United States tried to do to Iraq with conventional weapons in the Gulf War), the leader of a small nuclear power will feel incentives to delegate authority to alternative commanders in crises. Either policy increases the risks of accidents and unauthorized uses of nuclear weapons.

What is the evidence from new nuclear states? Good and bad news coexist here. On the positive side, some new nuclear nations—such as India and Pakistan—have thus far refrained from deploying alert weapons in peacetime, thus preferring to maintain "a bomb in the basement." This policy significantly reduces the risks of accidents and should be strongly encouraged, as I noted in Chapter 2. On the negative side, however, there are signs that new nuclear states are alerting their weapons in crises, using nuclear forces as signalling devices or preparing them for possible deliberate use in ways that also invariably raise the risks of accidental or unauthorized use. During the October 1973 Arab-Israeli war, for example, U.S. intelligence agencies picked up signals that Israel had started to placed its nuclear weapons on fighter-bomber aircraft, which were readied for immediate launch.[13] Similar, though not confirmed, reports exist that Israel also placed nuclear-tipped Jericho missiles on a high state of alert readiness during the Persian Gulf War in January 1991.[14] Finally, it has also been widely reported that U.S. intelligence agencies believed Pakistan assembled its nuclear weapons and began to load them onto alerted F-16 aircraft during the 1990 crisis over Kashmir; Soviet intelligence agencies reportedly also picked up similar signals of initial Indian nuclear weapons alert activities during that crisis.[15]

Third, Waltz argues that because new states, especially poor states, can "build sizable forces only over long periods of time, they have time to learn how to care for them" (Ch. 3, p. 97). This is true of some, but not of all new nuclear powers. Some, like the former republics of the USSR were born nuclear, inheriting very large nuclear arsenals rather than slowing building their own small arsenals. Indeed, on their first day as an independent state, Ukraine possessed an estimated 4,000 nuclear weapons, Kazakhstan some 1,400 weapons, and Belarus around 800 weapons.[16] Nuclear safety problems under such conditions in such states should hardly be surprising. Moreover, even for other more traditional cases of slower proliferation, learning to operate forces safely is not likely to be an easy task. Some states may gain valuable information from older nuclear powers: the United States reportedly shared some design information with France, and China reportedly was involved in the design of the Pakistani bomb.[17] Other states, however, are left to cope on their own and will experience more serious problems, as occurred in the Iraqi and South African cases. Finally, organizational learning is not just a matter of time and experience; it is also a matter of sharing information and blame, and therefore, the structure of political power within the state is important. In states in which civil-military relations are problematic or where the military is in power, there are likely to be strong inhibitions against organizational learning since this would require that the military services accept the blame for any accidents or near-accidents that occur.

Civilian Control and Preventive War

Waltz is clearly much less concerned than I am about the possibility that new nuclear powers will be the victims of a preventive attack by their neighbors or other adversaries. There are two related disagreements here. First, Waltz and I differ on preventive war because we differ on how quickly and with what degree of confidence new states will develop *what potential attackers* see as survivable second-strike forces. Second, we disagree over whether civilian and military leaders are likely to differ in their attitudes toward costs and benefits of preventive war once nuclear weapons are involved in the equation.

Waltz argues that preventive attacks are untenable because only a very small number of weapons are needed for deterrence. He therefore asserts that two or three weapons in North Korea will deter attacks and argues that the United States and the Soviet Union clearly had survivable second-strike forces in 1954, when the U.S. had some 1,500 weapons and the USSR had what the CIA estimated to be between one hundred-fifty and seven hundred weapons. What matters for stable deterrence, of course, is *not* what Kenneth Waltz, or Scott Sagan, or any other scholar thinks is a sufficient retaliatory force. What matters is what the decisionmakers of an adversary's state think. Looking at the large arsenals that existed in 1954, Waltz asks, "who would dare to strike forces of that size?" Well, quite a few people. As I noted in Chapter 2, many of the senior leaders of the U.S. military—Curtis LeMay, Orvil Anderson, Nathan Twining, Thomas Power, Thomas White, Hoyt Vandenberg, and Arthur Radford—advocated striking a preventive blow at the USSR during this period. Even as late as 1961, the chairman of the Joint Chiefs of Staff could tell President Kennedy that the United States would "prevail in [the] event of general nuclear war" with the USSR, even though the Soviet Union had what was then estimated to be an arsenal of approximately five hundred strategic nuclear weapons.[18]

The second disagreement is over whether civilians hold different views on the use of force. Waltz thinks that I worry too much about civilian control of the military in new nuclear states. (I agree with the general thrust of Waltz's first point in this section—that the United States has had problematic civil-military relations at times—yet I fail to see how this is comforting.) Waltz insists that military officers are not "more reckless and war-prone than civilian leaders" and presents a number of compelling examples. I agree in general, but not concerning the specific issue of *preventive war*.

Military officers certainly do tend to be highly conservative and cautious, as Waltz and I both note. Yet, that is precisely why they often have biases in favor of preventive war. Generals usually do not like war—"it spoils the army" one czarist officer said[19]—and often are highly opposed to military interventions; yet, if military officers believe that the use of force is necessary, they want to use it in as large and decisive a manner as possible. Here I would draw precisely the opposite lesson from the example that Waltz uses to show how conservative military planning works against preventive attacks. Waltz notes that the Tactical Air Command's senior commander, General Walter Sweeney could not promise to destroy 100 percent of the nuclear missiles found in Cuba during the 1962 crisis, but rather only 90 percent. What Waltz does not note, however, is that Sweeney nevertheless told President Kennedy that "he was certain that the air strike would be 'successful.'"[20] Indeed, despite the inability to strike all the missiles, the Joint Chiefs of Staff strongly urged the Kennedy administration to attack the sites immediately in a preventive strike on October 20th (before the missiles were deemed operational), and then again, on October 27, after the Soviet missiles became operational, the Joint Chiefs of Staff still recommended that the United States attack the sites and then invade Cuba.[21] The military was conservative and cautious all right, but that did not mean restraint: the inability to destroy all the missile sites in a first strike produced requests for multiple strikes and an invasion in order to ensure that the United States eventually destroyed all the Soviet missiles in Cuba.

Let me be very clear. Military officers are not more reckless or war-prone than are civilians. They often do, however, hold strong biases in favor of preventive war. The professional military, like members of any organization, have biases and blindspots. Military officers think that war is more likely in the long run than does the general population. Military officers, like members of other organizations, plan incrementally, which leads them to focus on achieving today's war aims, not on tomorrow's postwar problems. Like members of any organization, military officers focus on their narrow set of responsibilities, which limits their perspective and often produces very narrow definitions of success and victory.

In the final analysis, there is not too much that civilian authorities can do about these organizational level biases. Military organizations are boundedly rational because they are organizations. And ironically, military officers have limited perspectives in part because civilian leaders and publics want them to. Military professionals are trained to think in narrow ways: civilians do not want them to constrain their military advice because of political considerations, to contemplate the morals of their targeting plans, or to take the postwar world into deep consideration when planning attacks. Civilians want them to be professional soldiers, to make the most effective military plans possible, and to give stark and straightforward military advice. With respect to nuclear weapons, the result is that members of military organizations will more often advocate preventive war, will usually favor war-fighting doctrines, and will call for rapid escalation or none at all.

None of that should be particularly surprising or too disturbing. What is more disturbing is when such organizational biases are not successfully combatted by the checks and balances of strong civilian control. Bernard Brodie once wrote that "the civil hand must never relax, and must without one hint of apology hold the control that has always belonged to it by right."[22] Unfortunately, in this country, and especially in some new nuclear states with military-run or controlled governments, that civil hand is not always in firm control.

Second-Strike Forces

Waltz and I clearly disagree on how easy it will be for new states to build secure second-strike forces. What is the basis of this disagreement? I think Waltz's confident position is again built on logic of interests rather than the evidence of history. Of course, states will have interests in building survivable forces. But will they do so or will they screw up?

The answer is clear to Waltz: weak and poor states can build secure second-strike forces "quite easily" (Ch. 3, p. 108) and "they guard them with almost paranoic zeal" (Ch. 3, p. 97). In Chapter 2, I gave three recent counter-examples, showing how narrow organizational interests and poorly designed organizational routines can produce inadvertent and unnecessary vulnerabilities: first, the Chinese nuclear force was highly vulnerable in the mid-1970s, until Mao Zedong ordered that advanced deception plans be instituted; second, the Egyptian air force was destroyed in June 1967 because the Israelis noticed that all Egyptian air defense forces landed for refueling at the same time every morning; and third, in 1993, the North Korean construction of covert nuclear waste storage sites in a pattern identical to the sites found in Russia apparently helped the United States identify the location where the Koreans were hiding nuclear materials.

Here let me add that pre-nuclear history is filled with such examples of states zealously trying to guard valuable military assets, yet failing to do so. In 1941, the United States government desperately desired to protect the Pacific fleet at Pearl Harbor, because it was considered the central deterrent to war with Japan. The military alert plans of the army's anti-aircraft units were so focused on preventing sabotage, however, that when they received the warning to expect "hostile action" at any moment on November 27, they locked up their ammunition in storage bunkers, rather than distributing it to the gunners. The guns were thus silent when the Japanese attacked.[23] Nine hours later, despite having received warning that Pearl Harbor had been attacked, the critical B-17 "Flying Fortress" force at Clark Air Field in the Philippines was destroyed on the runway, because the bombers had earlier been launched into the air for protection upon receiving a false warning of Japanese aircraft approaching the base, and were in the process of refueling on the ground when the real attack came.[24] In late 1943, the German high command sought with zeal to hide the location of their V-1 buzz-bomb bases from the British; the V-1 storage buildings at every base, however, had been constructed in a distinctive curved shape (to protect the weapons inside from a bomb blast at the door), which looked like a ski from the air, enabling British photo-reconnaissance analysts to find ninety-five of the ninety-six bases constructed by the Germans.[25] Modern military history would look very different indeed if every time a state tried to protect its most critical military forces with zeal, it did so successfully.

Perhaps new nuclear states will do better. But in light of the evidence of history, one should not be surprised if some states fail to develop secure second-strike forces despite all hopes to the contrary. Imperfect organizations provide an imperfect link between desires of political leaders and the outcomes of force postures. These organizations make predictable (but not always preventable) mistakes. To ignore such organizational difficulties leads to serious misunderstandings, for both scholars trying to analyze the nuclear revolution and for statesmen trying to cope with its dangerous implications.

Imagining the Future

Waltz places great emphasis on the benefits of uncertainty regarding nuclear deterrence. Given the horrendous costs of an all-out war, states *should* be exceedingly cautious if there is *any* chance of nuclear weapons being involved. Yet nuclear uncertainty is a two-edged sword: it cuts against any absolute assurance that nuclear weapons *will not* be used (this helps deterrence) and also cuts against any absolute assurance that nuclear weapons *will* be used (this hurts deterrence).

How far does the nuclear writ run? History suggests that while many states facing nuclear adversaries may well be cautious, some states have nevertheless launched attacks in the face of such uncertainty. In 1973, Egypt and Syria attacked Israel despite the fact that Israel had a small nuclear arsenal at the time. In 1982, Argentina invaded the British-owned Falkland Islands, despite the fact that Great Britain had hundreds of nuclear weapons. In January 1991, during the Persian Gulf war, Iraq launched barrage after barrage of SCUD missiles into the cities of Israel, despite Israel having an estimated one hundred nuclear weapons and long-range Jericho missiles in its possession.[26] After the invasion of Kuwait, Prime Minister Yitzhak Shamir declared that "anyone attempting an attack on Israel will be bringing upon himself a great disaster."[27] How could Saddam Hussein have been *absolutely certain* that Israel would not retaliate with nuclear weapons? Governments take gambles, especially when they are in desperate straits. Nuclear weapons may well produce prudence, but it is a prudence that still leaves room for war.

Imagine the following scenario. What would happen if a resurgent Iraq develops or steals a handful of nuclear weapons in the future and then invades Kuwait again? Would the United States and other allied nations intervene? (We actually came within a few years of this scenario in 1991; had Saddam Hussein waited two or three more years before invading Kuwait, the Iraqi bomb would likely have been complete.[28]) The continuing spread of nuclear weapons will increase the likelihood of this kind of frightening possibility: small states can be more easily invaded by nuclear neighbors, since that neighbor may believe that its new weapons will deter intervention by outside powers. The United States and the international community at large may well face this problem in the next decade, if not in Iraq, then in Korea or Libya, or elsewhere.

Waltz appears quite sure that the United States would not launch an offense against a nuclear Iraq. An organizational perspective, however, leads me to be much less confident and to raise the following kinds of questions. What information would U.S. and allied decisionmakers have about the Iraqi weapons? *If* confident intelligence existed (accurate or otherwise) on where the weapons were located, there would be severe pressure to attack the sites as soon as possible before the weapons could be moved. What beliefs and plans would exist for fighting conventional wars in such cases? *If* U.S. decisionmakers and war planners believed that U.S. nuclear weapons deter other's use (just as some officials believed that U.S. nuclear weapons deterred the use of Saddam Hussein's chemical weapons arsenal in 1991[29]), a conventional invasion would be perceived as being an acceptable risk. What would happen next? Perhaps there would be a conventional war, as in 1991, without resort to nuclear weapons. Yet if a single Iraqi weapon went off by accident behind the front lines, would Iraqi military intelligence recognize this as an accident or report that a U.S. nuclear attack had started and call for retaliation? If an Iraqi bomb went off near U.S. troops, could U.S. intelligence agencies determine whether this was a deliberate or an accidental explosion, and how quickly? Certainly the pressure to "retaliate" massively and decisively, in an effort to destroy all possible weapon sites and command centers (and the surrounding areas) throughout Iraq, would be even more significant if there was a launch (whether it was a deliberate, or an accidental or unauthorized launch) of a nuclear-armed SCUD missile against Israel or U.S. forces.

I clearly do not know what the United States or other nations would do in such situations. Neither does Waltz. Nor for that matter does Bill Clinton or John Shalikashvili, or the political and military leaders of other countries. What can therefore be said with certainty? Not much. But that is the point. How confident can anyone be that states will always be deterred from conventional war simply because nuclear weapons use is possible? And how confident can anyone be that escalation will not occur despite hopes to the contrary?

IMAGINING THE PAST

It might not be difficult to envision how rapid escalation could occur if a large nuclear power enters a conventional war with a very small nuclear power. But what about a conflict between two states with relatively large nuclear arsenals? If small numbers of nuclear weapons are used, deliberately or accidentally, in such cases, would further escalation occur? Waltz's faith in nuclear deterrence is so strong that he believes it will reestablish itself even after it fails. "Should deterrence fail, a few judiciously delivered warheads are likely to produce sobriety in the leaders of all of the countries involved and thus bring rapid deescalation," he predicts (Ch. 1, p. 37). Indeed, he appears confident in retrospect that a nuclear war between the United States and the Soviet Union during the Cold War could have been rationally controlled. "Surely we would have struck military targets before striking industrial targets and industrial targets before striking cities. . . . The threat, if it failed to deter, would have been followed not by spasms of violence but by punishment administered in ways that conveyed threats of more to come." (Ch. 1, p. 35).

A deeper look inside U.S. military organizations and the operations they practiced and planned during the Cold War leads me to be highly skeptical about such views. Why? Even leaving aside the issue of whether there is any meaningful distinction between "industrial targets" and "cities" (there is not), three strong organizational reasons for skepticism exist. First, for much of the Cold War, U.S. nuclear war plans simply did not contain a meaningful option to permit such control to take place, even after civilian authorities requested such options. Despite Secretary of Defense Robert McNamara's 1960's guidance to the Joint Chiefs of Staff that the nuclear war

plan contain a "military-targets only" option (the counterforce option) to enhance escalation control, in the mid-
1970s Secretary of Defense James Schlesinger belatedly
discovered that the planned counterforce option con-
tained, in his words, "literally thousands of weapons"
and was therefore so large that "it was virtually indistin-
guishable from an attack on cities."[30] Second, we now
know of an important operational detail in the Strategic
Air Command (SAC) military machine that made perfect
discrimination in wartime unlikely even if the actual targeting plans had better reflected civilian desires. In the
1960s, SAC had a special switch called the "special
weapons emergency separation system" (SWESS) put
into its B-52 bombers so that the bombs would not be
"wasted" if the crewmen were killed in a wartime mission before they could get to their targets. The SWESS
system, once the switches were turned, would have
dropped and exploded U.S. nuclear bombs wherever the
SAC bombers happened to be when they descended be-
low 20,000 feet.[31] Thus, even if a U.S. president had ordered that only military targets be included in a limited
attack plan, the planned targets would not have been the
only ones destroyed. Third, U.S. operational war plans
were based entirely on the blast effects of nuclear weapons and did not, for organizational reasons, include the
effects of the large-scale fires that would be produced by
large nuclear weapons. Thus, even if only military targets were attacked, many nearby populated areas would
have been destroyed in the resulting firestorms.[32]

In short, it is extremely unlikely that the United
States could have fought a nuclear war against the Soviet
Union with the high degree of control and precision
imagined by Waltz.[33] Why expect that new states will do
any better? Perhaps the wishes of their leaders will be
more accurately implemented; perhaps their military will
not have biases in favor of large, decisive options; perhaps their war planners will not scrimp on safety to

maximize readiness; perhaps their leaders will place even greater importance on oversight of military operations than did such a notorious micro-manager as Robert McNamara. But I see no good reason to expect that such precise control over military operations will exist in weak nuclear states in the future when it did not exist in strong nuclear states in the past.

CONCLUSIONS

So what is to be done? The difficult nonproliferation challenge in the future is *not* to ensure that the U.S. government and people are opposed to the further proliferation of nuclear weapons. Indeed, it is not difficult to understand why a large nuclear state, with the most powerful conventional forces in the world, would want to limit severely the spread of nuclear weapons to other states in the international system. The real challenge is to create a future in which the government leaders, the organizations under them, and the citizens of nonnuclear states around the globe believe that it is in their interests to remain nonnuclear states.

This is clearly no easy task. Yet, despite the emergence of many new nuclear weapons states in the early 1990s, the recent history of nonproliferation efforts is not entirely bleak. Indeed, in the early 1990s, there were also a number of very important positive actions. Civilian-run governments in Argentina and Brazil gave up the nuclear weapons programs started by earlier military governments, preferring to enter an agreement for a nuclear-free zone in the region rather than face the uncertainties of a nuclear arms race.[34] South Africa built and fully assembled seven atomic explosive devices in the late 1970s and early 1980s, but then voluntarily dismantled and destroyed them after F. W. de Klerk came to power and started the process of ending apartheid and South Af-

rica's international isolation.[35] Three of the former republics of the Soviet Union—Belarus, Kazakhstan, and
Ukraine—agreed, after prolonged international negotia-
tions, to join the nuclear Non-Proliferation Treaty and to
return their weapons to Russia over the coming years,
where they will be dismantled and destroyed. In October
1994, North Korea agreed to permit full inspections of
their suspected nuclear weapons development facilities
in exchange for assistance in constructing advanced nuclear power reactors. The final inspections, however, will
not take place for another five years.

None of these apparent success stories is guaranteed
to last: treaties can be renounced, dismantlement discon-
tinued, and weapons programs renewed. Yet such positive developments should be encouraged and repro-
duced elsewhere when possible. In a world in which the
diffusion of nuclear power and weapons-related technologies is rampant, there is a very valuable lesson here.
In each of these examples, what changed was not the
supply of nuclear weapons materials, but rather the *de-
mand* for nuclear weapons. In each case, the states gave
up nuclear weapons when alternative security arrangements were deemed possible *and* when new political actors wanting changes in policy overcame the resistance of
other powerful actors and organizations.

Although international efforts to restrict access to
dangerous technologies should and will undoubtedly
continue, the United States can also play a very useful
role by helping to shape alternative security arrangements for potential nuclear states and new nuclear
states. For most potential states, the continuation of the
nuclear Non-Proliferation Treaty (NPT) in some form is
critical, since the treaty's system of inspection and verifi-
cation can produce strong assurances concerning
whether one's neighbors are producing the bomb or

whether mutual restraint is being followed. U.S. diplomacy can certainly encourage all nonnuclear states to maintain the NPT regime and to tighten its nuclear inspection procedures. Yet, perhaps most importantly, the U.S. can lead by its example: deeper reductions in U.S. arsenals could set a positive precedent for other powers; U.S. acceptance of a comprehensive test ban could reduce the belief in the developing world that the NPT is discriminatory; and U.S. adoption of what McGeorge Bundy, William Crowe, and Sidney Drell have called a "stringent doctrine of defensive last resort"[36] would focus increased opprobrium on states that maintain more offensive military doctrines and encourage the political forces for restraint within those states.

Ultimately, the key decisions will be made by the governments and peoples of new nuclear states and potential nuclear states, and not by the United States. Yet the visions of the future presented by officials and scholars in the United States are not utterly without influence. Looking out into the future, the goal of all states should not be a world of nuclear porcupines: every state sharply armed and vigorously trying to protect itself. Instead, the short-term goal should be radically smaller and safer arsenals in all existing nuclear states and maintenance of nonnuclear status for other nations. The long-term goal should be the abolition or international control of nuclear weapons, once appropriate political and technical controls can be devised.[37] I personally am not optimistic that I will ever see that goal achieved; but the difficulty of the task, and the distance we have to travel to achieve it, should not deter us from at least moving in the right direction. This is, in short, a time for creative efforts to combat proliferation, not for accepting the future spread of nuclear weapons as an inevitable or a positive development in international politics.

BACK TO THEORY

Theories are lenses. They help us focus on specific parts of a complex reality and see the causal connections between those parts. Theories help us understand the world; they enable us to make sense of the past and predict the future. Waltz and I use a different lens—neorealist structural theory and organization theory—to look at the same world. This has led us to emphasize different aspects of our nuclear history and to predict very different nuclear futures. Ultimately, the test of these different positions will be found in the experience of states that have acquired new nuclear weapons. I hope that Kenneth Waltz is right about the consequences of nuclear proliferation. I fear, however, that my more pessimistic predictions will eventually come true.

The awesome destructive power of nuclear weapons clearly increases the costs of war, and a statesman's awareness of this basic fact can be, in theory at least, a positive force for peace. But nuclear weapons are not controlled by states or statesmen; they are controlled by organizations. These organizations, like all complex organizations, will inevitably have biases and parochial interests, will by necessity develop routines and standardized procedures, and will occasionally make serious operational errors. The military's biases in favor of preventive war, common organizational problems in producing survivable forces, and inevitable imperfections in the safety of alert nuclear arsenals produced very serious problems for the superpowers during the Cold War. These kinds of problems are likely to reemerge, sometimes quietly and sometimes with a vengeance, in new nuclear nations. Nuclear weapons do not produce perfect nuclear organizations; they only make their inevitable mistakes more deadly. Because of the inherent limits of organizational reliability, the spread of nuclear weapons is more to be feared than welcomed.

NOTES

CHAPTER 1

1. Robert Jervis, "Cooperation under the Security Dilemma," *World Politics* 30 (January 1978). Cf. Malcolm Hoag, "On Stability in Deterrent Races," *World Politics* 13 (July 1961) and Stephen Van Evera, "Primed for Peace: Europe After the Cold War," *International Security* 15, no. 3 (Winter 1990–1991), p. 13.

2. Richard Smoke, *War: Controlling Escalation* (Cambridge: Harvard University Press, 1977), pp. 175-88.

3. Glenn H. Snyder, *Deterrence and Defense* (Princeton: Princeton University Press, 1961), p. 44; Van Evera, "Primed for Peace."

4. Snyder, *Deterrence and Defense*, pp. 37, 49, and 79-82; Bernard Brodie, *Escalation and the Nuclear Option* (Princeton: Princeton University Press, 1966), pp. 74–78; Robert Jervis, "Why Nuclear Superiority Doesn't Matter," *Political Science Quarterly* 94 (Winter 1979–80); Shai Feldman, *Israeli Nuclear Deterrence: A Strategy for the 1980s* (New York: Columbia University Press, 1982), *passim*.

5. Bernard Brodie, *War and Politics* (New York: Macmillan, 1973), p. 321.

6. Georg Simmel, "The Sociology of Conflict, I," *American Journal of Sociology* 9 (January 1904), p. 501.

7. George Sansom, "Japan's Fatal Blunder," in Robert J. Art and Kenneth N. Waltz, eds., *The Use of Force* (Boston: Little, Brown, 1971), pp. 208–209.

8. Cf. Lewis A. Dunn, "Nuclear Proliferation and World Politics," in Joseph I Coffey, ed., *Nuclear Proliferation: Prospects, Problems, and Proposals* (Philadelphia: The Annals of the American Academy of Political Science, March 1977), pp. 102-107. For a recent elaboration see Lewis A. Dunn, *Containing Nuclear Proliferation*, Adelphi Paper 263 (London: International Institute for Strategic Studies, 1991).

9. Dunn, "Nuclear Proliferation."

10. Feldman, *Israeli Nuclear Deterrence*, p. 163.

11. *The Middle East and North Africa, 1994*, 40th ed. (London: Europa Publications, 1993), pp. 363, 810.

12. For brief accounts, see S. E. Finer, *The Man on Horseback* (London: Pall Mall Press, 1962), pp. 106–108; and Roy Medvedev, "Soviet Policy Reported Reversed by SALT II," *Washington Star*, July 7, 1979, p. 1.

13. Cf. Kenneth N. Waltz, "America's European Policy Viewed in Global Perspective," in Wolfram F. Hanreider, ed., *The United States and Western Europe* (Cambridge, MA: Winthrop, 1974), p. 31; Richard K. Betts, *Soldiers, Statesmen, and Cold War Crises* (Cambridge: Harvard University Press, 1977), ap-

pendix A. For a revised version of this book with additional evidence from the Reagan and Carter administrations, see Betts, *Soldiers, Statesmen and Cold War Crises*, 2d ed. (New York: Columbia University Press, 1991).

14. Cf. John J. Weltman, "Nuclear Devolution and World Order," *World Politics* 32 (January 1980), pp. 190–92.

15. Cf. Dunn, "Nuclear Proliferation," p. 101.

16. The distinction between prevention—striking to prevent a state from gaining nuclear-military capability—and preemption—striking to destroy weapons before they can be used—is discussed in Chapter 3, pp. 103–106.

17. Walter H. Waggoner, "U.S. Disowns Matthews' Talk of Waging War to Get Peace," *New York Times*, August 27, 1950, p. 1.

18. William B. Bader, *The United States and the Spread of Nuclear Weapons* (New York: Pegasus, 1968), p. 96.

19. E.g., David M. Rosenbaum, "Nuclear Terror," *International Security* 1 (Winter 1977), p. 145.

20. See Kenneth N. Waltz, "Nuclear Myths and Political Realities," *American Political Science Review* 84, no. 3 (September 1990).

21. Geoffrey Kemp, *Nuclear Forces for Medium Powers: Part I: Targets and Weapons*, Adelphi Paper 196 (London: International Institute for Strategic Studies, 1974).

22. Justin Galen (pseud.), "US' Toughest Message to the USSR," *Armed Forces Journal International* (February 1979), p. 31.

23. Cf. Paul H. Nitze, "Assuring Strategic Stability in an Era of Detente," *Foreign Policy* 54, no. 2 (Winter 1976–77), pp. 207–32; James R. Schlesinger, "U.S.-U.S.S.R. Strategic Policies." Hearing before the Subcommittee on Arms Control, International Law and Organizations of the Committee on Foreign Relations, U.S. Senate, 93rd Cong., 2d sess., March 4, 1974, in Robert J. Pranger and Roger P. Labrie, eds., *Nuclear Strategy and National Security: Points of View* (Washington, DC: American Enterprise Institute, 1977), p. 105; Colin Gray, "Nuclear Strategy: A Case for a Theory of Victory," *International Security* 4 (Summer 1979), pp. 67–72.

24. Thomas C. Schelling, *The Strategy of Conflict* (New York: Oxford University Press, 1963), pp. 187–203.

25. Glenn H. Snyder, "Crisis Bargaining," in C. F. Hermann, ed., *International Crises: Insights from Behavioral Research* (New York: Free Press, 1972), p. 232.

26. John G. Stoessinger, *Henry Kissinger: The Anguish of Power* (New York: W. W. Norton, 1976), ch. 8.

27. Feldman, *Israeli Nuclear Deterrence*, pp. 29–32.

28. Steven J. Rosen, "Nuclearization and Stability in the Middle East," in Onkar Marwah and Ann Schultz, eds., *Nuclear Proliferation and the Near-Nuclear Countries* (Cambridge, MA: Ballinger, 1975), p. 173.

29. Frederic J. Brown, *Chemical Warfare: A Study in Restraints* (1968) in Art and Waltz, *The Use of Force*, p. 183.

30. Willaim T. R. Fox, "International Control of Atomic Weapons," in Bernard Brodie, ed., *The Absolute Weapon* (New York: Harcourt, Brace, 1946), p. 181.

31. Donald A. Quarles, "How Much Is Enough?" *Air Force* 49 (September 1956), pp. 51–52.

32. Harold Brown, Department of Defense, *Annual Report, FY 1980* (Washington, DC: GPO, 1980), pp. 75–76.

33. "Part II of the Press Conference by Valéry Giscard d'Estaing, President of the French Republic" (New York: French Embassy, Press and Information Division, February 15, 1979).

34. Eldon Griffiths, "The Revolt of Europe," *Saturday Evening Post* 263 (March 9, 1963), p. 19.

35. International Institute for Strategic Studies, *Strategic Survey* (London: Brassey's, various years).

36. Bernard Brodie, "War in the Atomic Age" in Brodie, *The Absolute Weapon*, p. 74.

37. Patrick Morgan, *Deterrence: A Conceptual Analysis* (Beverly Hills: Sage, 1977), p. 116.

38. Thomas C. Schelling, *Arms and Influence* (New Haven: Yale University Press, 1966), p. 22.

39. Richard Pipes, "Why the Soviet Union Thinks It Could Fight and Win a Nuclear War," *Commentary* 64, no. 1 (July 1977).

40. This section is based on Karen Ruth Adams and Kenneth N. Waltz, "Don't Worry Too Much About North Korean Nuclear Weapons," unpublished paper, April 1994.

41. John R. Wriggins, "CIA Plans Cutbacks, Spokesman Says," *Ellsworth American*, March 17, 1994, p. II-7.

42. Andrew K. Hanami, "Japan and the Military Balance of Power in Northeast Asia," *Journal of East Asian Affairs* 8, no. 2 (Summer 1994), p. 368.

43. International Institute for Strategic Studies, *Strategic Survey* (London: Brassey's, 1992–1993).

44. A. M. Rosenthal, "Always Believe Dictators," *New York Times*, March 29, 1994, p. A15.

45. R. W. Apple, "Facing Up to the Legacy of an Unresolved War," *New York Times*, June 12, 1994, p. E3.

46. John McCain, letter, *New York Times*, March 28, 1994, p. A10.

47. Eric Schmitt, "U.S. Is Redefining Nuclear Deterrence, Terrorist Nations Targeted," *International Herald Tribune*, February 26, 1993.

48. James Woolsey, "Proliferation Threats of the 1990's," Hearing before the Committee on Governmental Affairs, U.S. Senate, 103rd Cong., 1st sess., February 24, 1993 (Washington, DC: GPO, 1993), p. 134.

49. Claudia Dreifus, "Benazir Bhutto," *New York Times Magazine*, May 15, 1994, p. 39.

50. Shankar Bajpai, "Nuclear Exchange," *Far Eastern Economic Review*, June 24, 1993, p. 24.

51. Joseph Nye, "Maintaining a Non-Proliferation Regime," *International Organization* 35 (Winter 1981).

52. Feldman, *Israeli Nuclear Deterrence*, ch. 5.

53. Interviews by the author, December 1978.

54. Norman Angell, *The Great Illusion* (London: William Heinemann, 1914).

CHAPTER 2

1. References to Chapter 1 will appear in the text in parentheses (e.g., ch.1, p. x). References to Waltz's earlier work will appear in endnotes. Chapter 1 is a significantly revised and updated version of Waltz's 1981 analysis, which was published as Kenneth N. Waltz, *The Spread of Nuclear Weapons: More May Be Better*, Adelphi Paper 171 (London: International Institute for Strategic Studies, 1981).

2. Bruce Bueno de Mesquita and William H. Riker, "An Assessment of the Merits of Selective Nuclear Proliferation," *Journal of Conflict Resolution* 26, no. 2 (June 1982), p. 283.

3. John J. Mearsheimer, "Back to the Future: Instability in Europe After the Cold War," *International Security* 15, no. 1 (Summer 1990), pp. 5–56 (quote at p. 20) and Mearsheimer, "The Case for a Ukrainian Nuclear Deterrent," *Foreign Affairs* 72, no. 3 (Summer 1993), pp. 50–66. Mearsheimer's position on Japan was expressed on National Public Radio's "Morning Edition" on June 21, 1993. NPR Transcript, June 21, 1993, p. 21.

4. Stephen Van Evera, "Primed For Peace: Europe After the Cold War," *International Security* 15, no. 3 (Winter 1990/91), p. 54; Barry R. Posen, "The Security Dilemma and Ethnic Conflict," *Survival* 35, no. 1 (Spring 1993), pp. 44–45; Peter Lavoy, "Civil-Military Relations, Strategic Conduct, and the Stability of Nuclear Deterrence in South Asia," in *Civil-Military Relations and Nuclear Weapons* (Stanford Center for International Security and Arms Control, June 1994); Martin van Creveld, *Nuclear Proliferation and the Future of Conflict* (New York: Free Press, 1993); and Shai Feldman, *Israeli Nuclear Deterrence: A Strategy for the 1980s* (New York: Columbia University Press, 1982), pp. 142–75 and p. 238.

5. Important pessimistic appraisals include: Lewis A. Dunn, *Containing Nuclear Proliferation*, Adelphi Paper 263, (London: International Institute of Strategic Studies, 1991); Steven E. Miller, "The Case Against a Ukrainian Nuclear Deterrent," *Foreign Affairs* 72, no. 3 (Summer 1993), pp. 67–80; Paul Bracken, "Nuclear Weapons and State Survival in North Korea," *Survival* 35, no. 3 (Autumn 1993), pp. 137–53; and Peter D. Feaver, "Proliferation Optimism and Theories of Nuclear Operations," *Security Studies* 2, no. 3–4 (Spring/Summer 1993), pp. 159–91.

6. See, for example, the symposium on rational deterrence theory in *World Politics* 41, no. 2 (January 1989), pp. 143–224.

7. Kenneth N. Waltz, "Nuclear Myths and Political Realities," *American Political Science Review* 84, no. 3 (September 1990), p. 731 and p. 734. One measure of Waltz's influence on this issue is the fact that this article won the Heinz Eulau award for the best article published in the *APSR* in 1990.

8. Kenneth N. Waltz, "The Origins of War in Neorealist Theory," in Robert I. Rotberg and Theodore K. Rabb, eds., *The Origin and Prevention of Major Wars* (Cambridge, UK: Cambridge University Press, 1988), p. 50 and p. 51. Also see Waltz, "The Emerging Structure of International Politics," *International Security* 18, no. 2 (Fall 1993), pp. 51–55.

9. *Ibid* and Kenneth N. Waltz, "Response to My Critics," in Robert

O. Keohane (ed.) *Neorealism and Its Critics* (New York: Columbia University Press, 1986), p. 331.

10. Waltz, "Nuclear Myths and Political Realities," p. 739, (emphasis added).

11. The classic text is James G. March and Herbert Simon, *Organizations*, 2d ed. (Cambridge, MA: Basil Blackwell, 1993). For valuable reviews of relevant scholarship see Charles Perrow, *Complex Organizations*, 3rd ed. (New York: Random House, 1986), pp. 119–56 and Jonathan Bendor and Thomas H. Hammond, "Rethinking Allison's Models," *American Political Science Review* 86, no. 2 (June 1992), pp. 301–22

12. March and Simon, *Organizations*, p. 186. On goal displacement see Robert K. Merton, "Bureaucratic Structure and Personality," in Merton et al., eds., *Reader in Bureaucracy* (Glencoe, IL: Free Press, 1952), pp. 365–66; Herbert Simon "Bounded Rationality and Organizational Learning" *Organizational Science* 2, no. 1 (February 1991), pp. 125–34; and Charles Perrow, "Goals in Complex Organizations," *American Sociological Review* 26, no. 6 (December 1961), pp. 854–65.

13. The seminal works on conflict in organization theory are James G. March, "The Business Firm as a Political Coalition," *Journal of Politics* 24, no. 1 (February 1962), pp. 662–78; Richard M. Cyert and James G. March, *A Behavioral Theory of the Firm*, 2d ed. (Cambridge, MA: Basil Blackwell, 1992); and Philip Selznick, *TVA and the Grassroots* (Berkeley: University of California Press, 1949). For valuable recent perspectives, see Terry Moe, "Politics and the Theory of Organization," *Journal of Law, Economics, and Organization* 7 (special issue 1991), pp. 106–29; Jeffrey Pfeffer, *Power in Organizations* (Cambridge, MA: Ballinger, 1981); and James Q. Wilson, *Bureaucracy: What Government Agencies Do and Why They Do It* (New York: Basic Books, 1991), especially pp. 179–95.

14. Perrow, *Complex Organizations*, p. 132.

15. See Graham T. Allison, *Essence of Decision* (Boston: Little Brown, 1971); John D. Steinbruner, *The Cybernetic Theory of Decision* (Princeton: Princeton University Press, 1974); Morton H. Halperin, *Bureaucratic Politics and Foreign Policy* (Washington: Brookings, 1974); Barry R. Posen, *The Sources of Military Doctrine* (Ithaca: Cornell University Press, 1984); Bruce G. Blair. *The Logic of Accidental Nuclear War* (Washington: Brookings, 1993); and Scott D. Sagan, *The Limits of Safety: Organizations, Accidents and Nuclear Weapons* (Princeton: Princeton University Press, 1993).

16. For discussions of preventive war see Jack S. Levy, "Declining Power and the Preventive Motivation for War," *World Politics* 40, no. 1 (October 1987), pp. 82–107 and Randall L. Schweller, "Domestic Structure and Preventive War," *World Politics* 44, no. 2 (January 1992), pp. 235–69.

17. Waltz, *The Spread of Nuclear Weapons*, p. 12. Richard K. Betts, *Soldiers, Statesmen, and Cold War Crises*, 2d ed. (New York: Columbia University Press, 1991).

18. Samuel P. Huntington, *The Soldier and the State* (Cambridge, MA: Harvard University Press, 1957), p. 65 and Alfred Vagts, *Defense and Diplomacy: The Soldier and the Conduct of Foreign Relations* (New York: Crown Point Press, 1956), p. 263. For empirical support see John P. Lovell, "The Professional Socialization of the West Point Cadet," in Morris Janowitz,

ed., *The New Military* (New York: Russell Sage, 1964), p. 129 and Bengt Abrahamsson, "Military Professionalization and Estimates on the Probability of War," in Jacques van Doorn, ed., *Military Profession and Military Regimes* (The Hague: Mouton, 1969), pp. 35–51.

19. See Jack Snyder, *The Ideology of the Offensive* (Ithaca: Cornell University Press, 1984), pp. 26–30 and Posen, *The Sources of Military Doctrine*, pp. 47–50.

20. It is important to note, however, that Truman's military advisers tended to focus on tactical, military reasons for not using the bomb (such as the lack of suitable targets in Korea or the need to retain weapons for targets in the USSR), while civilians more often emphasized political factors (such as the effects on allied governments or U.S. public opinion). See John Lewis Gaddis, "The Origins of Self-Deterrence: The United States and the Non-Use of Nuclear Weapons, 1945–1958," in Gaddis, *The Long Peace: Inquires into the History of the Cold War* (New York: Oxford University Press, 1987), pp. 115–23 and Roger Dingman, "Atomic Diplomacy During the Korean War," *International Security* 13, no. 3 (Winter 1988/89), pp. 65–69.

21. The best source is Marc Trachtenberg's essay, "A 'Wasting Asset,' American Strategy and the Shifting Nuclear Balance, 1949–1954," in Trachtenberg, *History and Strategy* (Princeton: Princeton University Press, 1991), pp. 100–52.

22. SWNCC 282, "Basis for the Formulation of a U.S. Military Policy," September 19, 1945, reprinted in Thomas H. Etzold and John Lewis Gaddis, *Containment: Documents on American Policy and Strategy, 1945–1950* (New York: Columbia University Press, 1978), p. 42 (emphasis added). Significantly, the State Department's response to the report rejected the specific military recommendations that appeared "preventive in purpose." SC-169b, "Action on Joint Chiefs of Staff Statement on United States Military Policy," November 16, 1945, in *Ibid.*, p. 47.

23. "Text of Truman's `Report to Nation' on Korea War," *New York Times*, September 2, 1950, p. 4. Truman made similar comments in private conversations. For example, he told Admiral Leahy in May 1948 that the American people would never accept the bomb being used "for aggressive purposes." See David Alan Rosenberg, "American Atomic Strategy and the Hydrogen Bomb Decision," *Journal of American History*, vol. 66, no. 1 (June 1979), p. 67. Also see Harry S. Truman, *Years of Trial and Hope* (Garden City, NY: Doubleday, 1956), vol. 2, p. 359 and p. 383.

24. NSC-68, in *Foreign Relations of the United States* (hereinafter *FRUS* followed by year and volume), 1950, vol. 1, National Security Affairs, pp. 281–82. According to General Nathan Twining, the moral issue was the most important factor in NSC-68's rejection of preventive war. Nathan F. Twining, *Neither Liberty nor Safety* (New York: Holt, Rinehart and Winston, 1966), p. 49.

25. Anderson stated: "Give me the order to do it and I can break up Russia's five A-bomb nests in a week. . . . And when I went up to Christ—I think I could explain to Him that I had saved civilization." Austin Stevens, "General Removed over War Speech," *The New York Times*, September 2, 1950, p. 8.

26. See Trachtenberg, "A 'Wasting Asset,'" pp. 106–107 and p. 123;

and *USAF Basic Doctrine*, October 1951, K239.71605-1, Air Force Historical Research Center, Maxwell AFB, AL, p. 3.

27. Project Control suggested the following might be an appropriate definition of "aggression" calling for a U.S. military response after issuing the ultimatum: "Any nation that persists in the development and production of military force capable of threatening the existence of the Free World and whose political actions and stated national intent leaves no doubt that she intends to use military force to conquer or subjugate free countries should be considered as an aggressor who is preparing to commit an aggressive act against the United States." Quoted in Tami Davis Biddle, "Handling the Soviet Threat: 'Project Control' and the Debate on American Strategy in the Early Cold War Years," *The Journal of Strategic Studies* 12, no. 3 (September 1989), p. 287.

28. *Ibid*, pp. 291–92.

29. Matthew Ridgway, memorandum for the record, May 17, 1954, historical records file 1/15-6/30, Box 30, Ridgway papers, U.S. Army Military History Institute. Originally cited in David Alan Rosenberg, "The Origins of Overkill: Nuclear Weapons and American Strategy, 1945–1960," *International Security* 7, no. 4 (Spring 1983), p. 34.

30. Memorandum by the Chief of Staff, U.S. Air Force, to the JCS on The Coming National Crisis, (August 21, 1953), Twining Papers, series 2, topical series, nuclear weapons 1952-1961 folder, USAF Academy, Colorado Springs, CO.

31. Memorandum of Discussion, NSC meeting, November 24, 1954, *FRUS*, 1952–54, Vol. 2, National Security Affairs, part 1, p. 792.

32. In the future, Eisenhower wrote in a top secret memorandum to Dulles in September 1953, the U.S. "would have to be constantly ready, on an instantaneous basis, to inflict greater loss upon the enemy than he could reasonably hope to inflict on us. . . . This would be a deterrent—but if the contest to maintain this relative position should have to continue indefinitely, the cost would either drive us to war—or into some form of dictatorial government. In such circumstances, we would be forced to consider whether or not our duty to future generations did not require us to *initiate* war at the most propitious moment that we could designate." Memorandum by the President to the Secretary of State, September 8, 1953, *ibid*, p. 461 (emphasis in original).

33. Robert H. Ferrel (ed.), *The Diary of James C. Hagerty* (Bloomington. IN: University of Indiana Press, 1983), p. 69. Also see Trachtenberg, "A 'Wasting Asset'," p. 141 and McGeorge Bundy, *Danger and Survival: Choices about the Bomb in the First Fifty Years* (New York: Random House, 1988), p. 140.

34. When the U.S. preventive-war advocates presented their views in 1954, U.S. intelligence estimates of Soviet nuclear capabilities were highly uncertain, but nonetheless significant: estimates of the Soviet nuclear stockpile ranged from 188 to 725 nuclear weapons; and an estimated 300 Soviet bomber aircraft could be launched in a first strike, or possibly launched upon warning, of a U.S. attack, "200 to 250 of which might reach their targets [in the U.S.]." NIE 11-4-54 (August 28, 1954), Declassified Documents Reference System, 1981, No. 283A; and Memorandum by the Acting Special Assistant to the Secretary of State for Intelligence to the

Acting Secretary of State, (March 1, 1954), *FRUS*, 1952-1954, Vol. 2, National Security Affairs, part 1, p. 634.

35. Although advocacy of preventive war diminished within the U.S. military in the late 1950s, common organizational proclivities continued to influence military thinking about nuclear war. Goal displacement was especially pronounced in the early integrated war plans which enabled the JCS to argue, as late as 1961, that the U.S. would "prevail in the event of general nuclear war," even if the USSR struck first. Prevail in this context did *not* mean avoiding massive U.S. casualties, however; it simply meant achieving the damage expectancy war aims set out in the guidance given to war planners. See Scott D. Sagan, "SIOP-62: The Nuclear War Plan Briefing to President Kennedy," *International Security* 12, no. 1 (Summer 1987), p. 36.

36. Estimates of the size and status of the Indian and Pakistani weapons arsenals are very uncertain. One conservative estimate is that Pakistan could produce about eight bombs today, while India has the material to construct approximately fifty bombs. See Brahma Chelleney, "The Challenge of Nuclear Arms in South Asia," *Survival* 35, no. 3 (Autumn 1993), pp. 124–25.

37. Stephen P. Cohen, *The Pakistan Army* (Berkeley, CA: University of California Press, 1984), p. 112.

38. On the preventive motivations for Pakistan's 1965 attack see *Ibid*, p. 139 and Sumit Ganguly, *The Origins of War in South Asia* (Boulder, CO: Westview Press, 1986), pp. 57–95.

39. Richard Sisson and Leo Rose, *War and Secession: Pakistan, India, and the Creation of Bangladesh* (Berkeley, CA: University of California Press, 1990), pp. 276–77. Some scholars view Pakistan's 1971 attack against India as a preventive war, although it is a less clear-cut case since limited numbers of Indian forces had covertly intervened in the civil conflict in Bengal prior to Pakistan's major offensive. See *Ibid*, pp. 227–30; Cohen, *The Pakistan Army*, p. 145; and Fazal Muqeem Khan, *Pakistan's Crisis in Leadership* (Islamabad, Pakistan: National Book Foundation, 1973), pp. 192–94.

40. On the 1990 crisis see John M. Broder and Stanley Meisler, "Terrifying Pursuit of Nuclear Arms," *Los Angeles Times*, January 19, 1992, p. A1 and Seymour M. Hersh, "On the Nuclear Edge," *The New Yorker*, March 29, 1993, pp. 56–73. Hersh quotes (p. 65) an unidentified U.S. intelligence source as follows: "They had F-16s prepositioned and armed for delivery—on full alert, with pilots on the aircraft. I believed that they were ready to launch on command." The U.S. military attaché in Pakistan in 1990, however, has denied that the United States had any evidence that F-16s were alerted during the crisis. See Michael Krepon and Mishi Faruqee, eds., *Conflict Prevention and Confidence Measures in South Asia: The 1990 Crisis* (Washington, DC: Stimson Center Occasional Paper 17, 1994), p. 21.

41. Stephen Foye, "Civilian-Military Tensions in Ukraine," *Radio Free Europe/Radio Liberty Research Report* 2, no. 5, (June 18, 1993), p. 66.

42. Paul Quinn-Judge, "Yeltsin Weighed Nuclear Strike on Ukraine, Soviet Report Says," *Boston Globe*, October 25, 1991, p. 10 and "'Nuclear Strike' Rumors Blamed on Media, Yeltsin," *Izvestiya*, October 25, 1991, FBIS-SOV-91-207, October 25, 1991, p. 17.

43. See William C. Martel and William T. Pendley, *Nuclear Coexistence: Rethinking U.S. Policy to Promote Stability in an Era of Proliferation*, Air War College, (Maxwell AFB, AL), Studies in National Security No. 1, (April 1994), p. 58.

44. Mearsheimer, "The Case for a Ukrainian Nuclear Deterrent," p. 58.

45. Posen, "The Security Dilemma and Ethnic Conflict," p. 39.

46. On Soviet planning during the crisis see Bruce G. Blair, *The Logic of Accidental Nuclear War* (Washington, DC: Brookings, 1993), p. 25 and Raymond L. Garthoff, *Detente and Confrontation* (Washington, DC: Brookings, 1985), p. 209. According to Arkady Shevchenko, Defense Minister Andrei Grechko advocated preventive war against China in 1969, while first deputy chief of the General Staff, General Nicolai Orgarkov was more restrained. Arkady Shevchenko, *Breaking With Moscow* (New York: Knopf, 1985), p. 165.

47. See Michael C. Desch, "Why the Soviet Military Supported Gorbachev, but Why the Russian Military Might Only Support Yeltsin for a Price," *Journal of Strategic Studies* 16, no. 4 (December 1993) and Robert Arnett, "Russia After the Crisis: Can Civilians Control the Military?" *Orbis* 38, no. 1 (Winter 1994), pp. 44–57.

48. See John Morrison, "Yeltsin: Generals Balked at My Order," *San Francisco Chronicle*, April 24, 1994, p. A-6.

49. Waltz, "Nuclear Myths and Political Realities," p. 732.

50. *Ibid.*," p. 731; Waltz, "Origins of War in Neorealist Theory," p. 51.

51. Halperin, *Bureaucratic Politics and Foreign Policy*, p. 28.

52. See Henry S. Rowen and Richard Brody, "The Development of U.S. Nuclear Strategy and Employment Policy," in Andrew W. Marshall et al., eds., *On Not Confusing Ourselves* (Boulder, CO: Westview Press, 1991) p. 32 and Fred Kaplan, *The Wizards of Armageddon* (New York: Simon and Schuster, 1983), p. 99.

53. Bruce L. R. Smith, *The RAND Corporation* (Cambridge: Harvard University Press, 1966), pp. 222–23.

54. *Ibid.*, p. 226.

55. Harvey M. Sapolsky, *The Polaris System Development* (Cambridge, MA: Harvard University Press, 1972), p. 15.

56. *Ibid.*, pp. 17–18. Opposition also existed because another navy tradition—that ships should only have one commanding officer—was also challenged by the development of ballistic missile submarines which used two commanders and crews, so that replacements could take over immediately after a lengthy patrol at sea. *Ibid.*, p. 35.

57. *Ibid.*, p. 18. Also see Vincent Davis, *The Politics of Innovation: Patterns in Navy Cases*, University of Denver Monograph Series in World Affairs 4, no. 3 (1966–67), p. 23.

58. Edmund Beard, *Developing the ICBM* (New York: Columbia University Press, 1976), p. 8.

59. Robert Frank Futrell, *Ideas, Concepts, Doctrine: A History of Basic Thinking in the United States Air Force* (Maxwell AFB, AL: Air University, 1971), p. 257; Beard, *Developing the ICBM*, p. 85.

60. Beard, *Developing the ICBM*, pp. 153–94.

61. See John Wilson Lewis and Hua Di, "China's Ballistic Missile Programs: Technologies, Strategies, and Goals," *International Security* 17, no. 2 (Fall 1992), pp. 18–19 and p. 28.

62. Chong-Pin Lin, *China's Nuclear Weapons Strategy* (Lexington, MA: Lexington Books, 1988), p. 64; He Chiang, "PRC Ballistic Missiles: A Preliminary Survey," *Conmilit* 2, no. 7 (August 1978), p. 12, as quoted in *Ibid.*, p. 63.

63. Lewis and Hua, "China's Ballistic Missile Programs," p. 24.

64. *Ibid.*, p. 12 and p. 27.

65. Nadav Safran, *From War to War* (New York: Pegasus, 1969) p. 319.

66. *New York Times*, May 26, 1967, p. 16. Also see Anthony Nutting, *Nasser* (New York: E. P. Dutton, 1972), p. 398.

67. Edgar O'Ballance, *The Third Arab-Israeli War* (Hamden, CN: Archon Books, 1972), p. 65. This is not a uncommon problem. Despite assurances to the contrary, U.S. aircraft at bases in Florida were discovered to be deployed wing-tip to wing-tip at the height of the Cuban missile crisis. See Allison, *Essence of Decision*, p. 139 and *Chronology of JCS Decisions Concerning the Cuban Crisis*, Historical Division, Joint Chiefs of Staff, December 21, 1962 (National Security Archives, Washington, D.C.), pp. 31–32 and pp. 40–41.

68. O'Ballance, *The Third Arab-Israeli War*, p. 63 and Safran, *From War to War*, p. 321.

69. David Albright, "How Much Plutonium Does North Korea Have?" *Bulletin of Atomic Scientists* 50, no. 5 (September/October 1994), p. 48.

70. See Allison, *Essence of Decision*, p. 107..

71. The best examples of "high reliability theory" are Joseph G. Morone and Edward J. Woodhouse, *Averting Catastrophe: Strategies for Regulating Risky Technologies* (Berkeley: University of California Press, 1986); Todd R. La Porte and Paula M. Consolini, "Working in Practice But Not in Theory: Theoretical Challenges of 'High Reliability Organizations,'" *Journal of Public Administration Research and Theory* 1, no. 1 (January 1991), pp. 19–47; Karlene H. Roberts, ed., *New Challenges to Understanding Organizations* (New York: Macmillan, 1993); Aaron Wildavsky, *Searching For Safety* (New Brunswick, N.J.: Transaction Books, 1988); and Jonathan B. Bendor, *Parallel Systems: Redundancy in Government* (Berkeley: University of California Press, 1985).

72. Charles Perrow, *Normal Accidents: Living with High-Risk Technologies* (New York: Basic Books, 1984), *passim*.

73. These ideas and the examples that follow are discussed in more detail in Sagan, *The Limits of Safety*.

74. For further discussion see Scott D. Sagan, "Toward a Political Theory of Organizational Reliability," *The Journal of Contingencies and Crisis Management* 2, no. 4 (December 1994).

75. Communications from the Thule radar would go dead, the bomb alarm would report a detonation, and efforts to contact the B-52 would not succeed.

76. Gary Milhollin, "Building Saddam Hussein's Bomb," *New York Times Magazine*, March 8, 1992, p. 32.

77. See Avner Cohen and Benjamin Frankel, "Opaque Nuclear Proliferation," *Journal of Strategic Studies* 13, no. 3 (September 1990), p. 34 and Feaver, "Proliferation Optimism and Theories of Nuclear Operations," pp. 175–78.

78. As Brahma Chellaney has noted: "In theory, India's atomic energy complex is under the control of the Indian cabinet and top civil servants of the Cabinet Secretariat and is answerable to the national parliament. In practice, however, the complex, with its burgeoning bureaucracy, operates on its own." Brahma Chellaney, "The Challenge of Nuclear Arms Control in South Asia," *Survival* 35, no. 3 (Autumn 1993), p. 127.

79. *Weapons Proliferation in the New World Order*, Hearing before the Committee on Governmental Affairs, U.S. Senate, 102nd Cong., 2d sess., January 15, 1992, p. 25. According to the *Economist's* newsletter, *Foreign Report*, "America has made sure that electrical connections for making the bomb ready in mid-flight have not been delivered. . . . That might offend safety standards in the American air force, but Pakistan's standards are probably lower." *Foreign Report*, January 12, 1989, p. 2.

80. See Victor Litovkin, "Second Chernobyl Brewing in Ukraine's Missile Silos," *Izvestiya*, February 16, 1993, FBIS-SOV-029, February 19, 1993, p. 1; "Russian says Ukraine Strengthening Control over Nuclear Arms," Moscow UPI Press Report, September 14, 1993 and "Russia Refuses to Recognize Ukraine's START I Ratification," Moscow UPI Press Report, November 26, 1993. Also see Christoph Bluth, " Strategic Nuclear Weapons and US-Russian Relations," *Contemporary Security Policy* 15, no. 1 (April 1994), pp. 92–95.

81. "2 Leaky Nuclear Warheads Cause Worry as Ukraine, Russia Bicker," *The San-Diego Union-Tribune*, October 20, 1993, p. A-12.

82. See Jessica Eve Stern, "Moscow Meltdown: Can Russia Survive," *International Security* 18, no. 4 (Spring 1994).

83. William Potter, "Nuclear Threats from the Former Soviet Union," Center for Security and Technology Studies, Lawrence Livermore National Laboratory, March 16, 1993, p. 6.

84. See Leonard S. Spector, *Going Nuclear* (Cambridge, MA: Ballinger, 1987), pp. 25–32.

85. John Wilson Lewis and Xue Litai, *China Builds the Bomb* (Stanford: Stanford University Press, 1988), pp. 202–203.

86. See especially Hans J. Morgenthau, *Defending the National Interest* (New York: Knopf, 1951) and George F. Kennan, *American Diplomacy* (Chicago: University of Chicago Press, 1951).

87. Kenneth N. Waltz, *Theory of International Politics* (New York: Random House, 1979), p. 118. In his 1986 essay Waltz similarly argued that "the international system is a competitive one in which the less skillful must expect to pay for their ineptitude. The situation provides enough incentive to cause *most of the actors* to behave sensibly." Waltz, "Response to My Critics," p. 331, (emphasis added).

88. Waltz, "Response to My Critics," p. 331.

89. Fortunately, a new wave of scholarship is starting to use and

contribute to organization theory in an effort to understand major problems of international security. For examples, see: Deborah D. Avant, "The Institutional Sources of Military Doctrine: Hegemons in Peripheral Wars," *International Studies Quarterly* 37, no. 4 (December 1993) pp. 409–30; Sun-Ki Chai, "An Organizational Economics Theory of Antigovernment Violence," *Comparative Politics* 26, no. 1 (October 1993), pp. 99–110; Chris C. Demchak, *Military Organizations, Complex Machines* (Ithaca: Cornell University Press, 1991); Peter D. Feaver, *Guarding the Guardians* (Ithaca: Cornell University Press, 1992); Jeffrey W. Legro, "Military Culture and Inadvertent Escaltion in World War II," *International Security* 18, no. 4 (Spring 1994), pp. 108–42; Robert L. Kahn and Mayer N. Zald, eds., *Organizations and Nations-States* (San Francisco: Jossey-Bass, 1990); Elizabeth Kier, *Imagining War: British and French Military Doctrine before World War II* (Princeton: Princeton University Press, forthcoming); Donald MacKenzie, *Inventing Accuracy: A Historical Sociology of Nuclear Missile Guidance* (Cambridge, MA: MIT Press, 1990); Marc C. Suchman and Dana P. Eyre, "Military Procurement as Rational Myth: Notes on the Social Construction of Weapons Proliferation," *Sociological Forum* 7, no. 1 (March 1992), pp. 137–61; and Kimberly Martin Zisk, *Engaging the Enemy: Organization Theory and Soviet Military Innovation* (Princeton: Princeton University Press, 1993).

90. For example see the discussions of Waltz and Mearsheimer in Ravi Shastri, "Developing Nations and the Spread of Nuclear Weapons," *Strategic Analysis* (New Delhi), 11, no. 12 (March 1988), pp. 1379–91 and "Kiev and the Bomb: Ukrainians Reply," *Foreign Affairs* 72, no. 4 (September/October 1993), pp. 183–86.

91. The best analysis of U.S. options is Steven E. Miller, "Assistance to Newly Proliferating Nations," in Robert D. Blackwell and Albert Carnesale, eds. *New Nuclear Nations* (New York: Council on Foreign Relations, 1993), pp. 97–131.

92. A detailed discussion of U.S. nuclear weapons safety mechanisms appears in Sidney Drell and Bob Peurifoy, "Technical Issues of a Nuclear Test Ban," *Annual Review of Nuclear and Particle Science* 44, (December 1994), pp. 294–313.

CHAPTER 3

1. Bertolt Brecht, *Mother Courage and Her Children: A Chronicle of the Thirty Years' War*, trans. Eric Bentley (New York: Grove Press, 1966), p. 76. C. P. Snow, "Excerpts from Snow's Speech to American Scientists," *New York Times*, December, 28, 1960, p. 14.

2. Bruce G. Blair and Henry W. Kendall, "Dismantle Armageddon," *New York Times*, May 21, 1994, p. 21. Also see Scott D. Sagan, *The Limits of Safety: Organizations, Accidents, and Nuclear Weapons* (Princeton: Princeton University Press, 1993), pp. 225–49.

3. Bruce G. Blair and Henry W. Kendall, "Accidental Nuclear War," *Scientific American* 263, no. 6 (December 1990), p. 53; and Sagan, *The Limits of Safety*, pp. 275–77.

4. Walter Millis, ed., *The Forrestal Diaries* (New York: Viking Press, 1951), pp. 492–530; and Warner R. Schilling, "Conclusions," in Warner R. Schilling, Paul Y. Hammond, and Glenn H. Snyder (eds.), *Strategy, Politics and Defense Budgets* (New York: Columbia University Press, 1962), p. 217.

5. David Alan Rosenberg, "A Smoking, Radiating Ruin at the End of Two Hours: Documents of American Plans for Nuclear War with the Soviet Union, 1954–1955," *International Security*, Vol. 6 (Winter 1981–82).

6. Stephen E. Ambrose, *Eisenhower: Soldier and President* (New York: Simon and Schuster, 1990), p. 543.

7. "The No-Cities Doctrine," in Robert J. Art and Kenneth N. Waltz, *The Use of Force: Military Power and International Politics*, 4th ed. (Lanham, MD: University Press of America, 1993), p. 376.

8. See, for example, Schillings' discussion of Medaris, Taylor, Gavin, and Ridgeway, in *Strategy, Politics and Defense Budgets*, pp. 229 and 242–43. On Taylor, see Colonel James A. Donovan, *Militarism, U.S.A.* (New York: Scribner's, 1970), pp. 119–20; General Maxwell Taylor, *The Uncertain Trumpet* (New York: Harper and Brothers, 1960); General Matthew Ridgway, *Soldier* (New York: Harper and Brothers, 1956); Major General J. B. Medaris, *Countdown for Decision* (New York: Paperback Library, 1961).

9. Alfred Vagts, *A History of Militarism: Civilian and Military* (New York: Free Press, 1959), p. 165.

10. Elaine Sciolino, "Clinton's Haiti Problem: What Price Democracy?" *New York Times*, July 7, 1994, p. A8.

11. Richard H. Kohn, "Out of Control," *The National Interest*, no. 35 (Spring 1994), pp.12–13, 17.

12. Kenneth N. Waltz, "A Necessary War?" *Confrontation in the Gulf* (Berkeley: Institute of International Studies, 1992), pp. 59–65.

13. The German armies in the west in 1940 had 136 divisions against 156 French, British, Belgian, and Dutch divisions. The Germans had 2,800 tanks and faced more than 4,000. Klaus Knorr, *The War Potential of Nations* (Princeton: Princeton University Press, 1963), pp. 30–31.

14. Bernard Brodie, *Strategy in the Missile Age* (Princeton: Princeton University Press, 1959), p. 275

15. William J. Broad, "Book Says Britain Bluffed about Its H-Bombs," *New York Times*, March 24, 1994, p. A 4.

16. Kenneth N. Waltz, "Nuclear Myths and Political Realities," *American Political Science Review* 84, no. 3 (September 1990).

17. Robert McNamara, "Reducing the Risk of Nuclear War: Is Star Wars the Answer?" *Millennium: Journal of International Studies* 15, no. 2 (Summer 1986), p. 137.

18. Cited in Robert L. Gallucci, "Limiting U.S. Policy Options to Prevent Nuclear Weapons Proliferation: The Relevance of Minimum Deterrence," Center for Technical Studies on Security, Energy and Arms Control, Lawrence Livermore National Laboratory, February 28, 1991, p. 6.

19. Waltz, "Nuclear Myths and Political Realities."

20. Henry Kissinger, *For the Record: Selected Statements, 1977–1980* (Boston: Little, Brown, 1981), p. 18.

21. Scott Sagan has managed to find three, not all of which are unambiguous, *Limits of Safety*, p. 263.

22. Editorial, "Disarming the Subcontinent," *New York Times*, March 29, 1994, p. A 14.

23. Steven Erlanger, "Ukraine's Hedging on A-Arms," *New York Times*, November 22, 1993, p. A 3.

24. Desmond Ball concludes that with strategic warheads a war could not be sustained beyond the shooting of weapons numbered in the tens: "Counterforce Targeting: How New? How Viable?" *Arms Control Today* 11, p. 9.

25. Blair and Kendall, "Accidental Nuclear War," p. 53; Cf. Von Hippel et al., "How to Avoid Nuclear War," *Bulletin of the Atomic Scientists* 46, no. 5 (June 1990), pp. 35–36.

CHAPTER 4

1. For detailed analyses of the nuclear revolution see Charles L. Glaser, *Analyzing Strategic Nuclear Policy* (Princeton, NJ: Princeton University Press, 1990); and Robert Jervis, *The Meaning of the Nuclear Revolution* (Ithaca, NY: Cornell University Press, 1989). During the Cold War, I argued that it was possible and desirable to develop a "second-strike counterforce" capability to enhance deterrence at an organizational level, by preventing Soviet military planners from achieving their targeting war aims, and thus not even achieve their narrow definition of victory. I argued, however, that such a capability could be smaller in size, safer in operations, and slower in arrival than the U.S. arsenal developed in the 1980s. See Scott D. Sagan, *Moving Targets: Nuclear Strategy and National Security* (Princeton, NJ: Princeton University Press, 1989), pp. 58–97.

2. See the evidence presented in Joseph G. Morone and Edward J. Woodhouse, *The Demise of Nuclear Energy?* (New Haven, CT: Yale University Press, 1989); and Joseph V. Rees, *Hostages to Each Other: The Transformation of Nuclear Safety Since Three Mile Island* (Chicago: University of Chicago Press, 1994).

3. On the organizational roots of the space shuttle Challenger accident see, Diane Vaughan, *The Challenger Launch Decision: Risk, Culture, and Deviance at NASA* (Chicago: University of Chicago Press, forthcoming 1995); C.f. Larry Heimann, "Understanding the *Challenger* Disaster: Organizational Structure and the Design of Reliable Systems," *American Political Science Review* 87, no. 2 (June 1993), pp. 421–35; and William H. Starbuck and Francis J. Milliken, "*Challenger:* Fine-Tuning the Odds until Something Breaks," *Journal of Management Studies* 25, no. 4 (July 1988), pp. 319–40.

4. See Scott D. Sagan, "Toward a *Political* Theory of Organizational Reliability," *Journal of Contingencies and Crisis Management* 2, no. 4 (December 1994) and James F. Short and Lee Clarke, eds., *Organizations, Uncertainties, and Risk* (Boulder, CO: Westview Press, 1992).

5. See Bruce G. Blair, *The Logic of Accidental Nuclear War* (Washington, DC: Brookings, 1993); Paul Bracken, *Command and Control of Nuclear Forces* (New Haven, CT: Yale University Press, 1983); Peter Douglas Feaver, *Guarding the Guardians: Civilian Control of Nuclear Weapons in the United States* (Ithaca, NY: Cornell University Press, 1992); and Scott D. Sagan, *The Limits of Safety: Organizations, Accidents, and Nuclear Weapons* (Princeton, NJ: Princeton University Press, 1993).

6. John R. Harvey and Stefan Michalowski, "Nuclear Weapons Safety: The Case of Trident," *Science and Global Security* 4, no. 3 (1994) pp. 261–338 .

7. Sidney Drell and Bob Peurifoy, "Technical Issues of a Nuclear Test Ban," *Annual Review of Nuclear and Particle Science* 44 (December 1994), pp. 285–327.

8. Let me give a few examples. In the fall of 1992, several sabotage incidents were discovered at the main plutonium facility at the Los Alamos National Laboratory, which could have produced, according to the Department of Energy, "a fire-induced or explosion-induced release of plutonium." In December 1993, a General Accounting Office study discovered that technicians at the Pantex weapons plant had recently dropped one

nuclear weapons core and had accidentally permitted radioactive gas to escape from another. In October 1994, the U.S. government shut down most operations at its only facility for handling the uranium from disassembled nuclear weapons after outside inspectors discovered "hundreds of safety violations" there. In November 1993, three officers from the Russian Northern Fleet broke into a fuel rod storage depot and stole 4.5 kilograms of enriched uranium, hoping to sell it on the black market. In August 1994, German authorities reported that more than 500 grams of plutonium was seized as it was being smuggled out of Russia. See Office of Nuclear Safety, Department of Energy, *New Directions in Nuclear Safety Management and Organization*, April 2, 1993, p. 35; Matthew L. Wald, "Study Faults U.S. Program to Dismantle Atomic Arms," *New York Times*, December 1, 1993, p. A12; Matthew L. Wald, "Disassembly of A-Bombs Stopped After Inspectors Find Violations," *New York Times*, October 4, 1994, p. A1; Nicolay Rodionov, "The Stolen Uranium Would Have Been Enough to Make a Nuclear Bomb," *Segodnya* (Moscow), July 2, 1994 in Foreign Broadcast Information Service (FBIS-SOV-94-128), July 5, 1994, p. 27; and Craig Whitney, "Germans Seized Third Atomic Sample Smuggled by Plane from Russia," *New York Times*, August 14, 1994, p. A1.

9. Gary Milhollin, "Building Saddam Hussein's Bomb," *New York Times Magazine*, March 8, 1992, p. 32. Also see David Albright and Mark Hibbs, "Iraq's Bomb: Blueprints and Artifacts," *Bulletin of Atomic Scientists* 48, no. 1 (January/February 1992), pp. 30–40.

10. David Albright, "South Africa's Secret Nuclear Weapons," *ISIS Report* (Institute for Science and International Security) 1, no. 4 (May 1994), p. 10.

11. See Albert Carnesale, "Defenses Against New Nuclear Threats," in Robert D. Blackwell and Albert Carnesale, eds., *New Nuclear Nations* (New York: Council on Foreign Relations, 1994), pp. 196–215.

12. For valuable discussions of the trade-offs between actions designed to increase the certainty of deliberate use and those designed to decrease the risks of accidents and unauthorized use, see Peter D. Feaver, "Command and Control in Emerging Nuclear States," *International Security* 17, no. 3, (Winter 1992–93), pp. 160–87; and Bradley A. Thayer, "The Risk of Nuclear Inadvertence: A Review Essay," *Security Studies* 3, no. 3 (Spring 1994), pp. 428–93.

13. This alert was reported by Seymour M. Hersh in *The Samson Option: Israel's Nuclear Arsenal and American Foreign Policy* (New York: Random House, 1991), p. 231. U.S. knowledge of the Israel alert was confirmed by a former National Security Council official, William B. Quandt, in his review essay, "How Far Will Israel Go," *Washington Post Book World*, November 24, 1991.

14. For reports that Israel alerted its nuclear arsenal during the 1991 Gulf War see Hersh, *The Samson Option*, p. 318 and Bill Gertz, "Israel Deploys Missiles for a Possible Strike at Iraq," *Washington Times*, January 28, 1991, p. B-7. Other sources have claimed, however, that the United States did not receive any intelligence on an Israeli nuclear weapons alert. See "Special Report: The Secret History of the War," *Newsweek*, March 18, 1991, p. 36.

15. James Adams, "Pakistan 'Nuclear War Threat,'" *Sunday Times*

(London), May 27, 1990, p. A-1 and John M. Broder and Stanley Meisler, "Terrifying Pursuit of Nuclear Arms," *Los Angeles Times,* January 19, 1992, p. A-1. The retired Pakistani army chief of staff denied that such alert activities took place and blamed "the Indian lobby" for misleading U.S. intelligence agencies. In contrast, a senior Indian government official stated that the United States told New Dehli that U.S. spy satellites had picked up indications of a Pakistani nuclear alert, *after* the 1990 crisis was resolved and that India did not alert its forces in response. See Mirza Aslam Beg, "Who Will Press the Button?" *Saudi Gazette* (May 8, 1994) reprinted in *Moneyclips,* May 8, 1994; and Raju Gopalakrishnan, "Indian Official Denies Threat of Nuclear War," Reuters News Service, March 22, 1993.

16. The estimates are from the National Resources Defense Council. See Robert S. Norris, "The Soviet Nuclear Archipelago," *Arms Control Today* (January/February 1992), p. 25.

17. On the U.S. sharing see Richard H. Ullman, "The Covert French Connection," *Foreign Policy,* no. 75 (Summer 1989), pp. 3–33. On China's assistance to Pakistan see David Albright and Mark Hibbs, "Pakistan's Bomb: Out of the Closet," *Bulletin of Atomic Scientists* 48, no. 6 (July/August 1992), pp. 42–43.

18. See Scott D. Sagan, "SIOP-62: The Nuclear War Plan Briefing to President Kennedy," *International Security* 12, no. 1 (Summer 1987), p. 36.

19. As quoted in Samuel P. Huntington, *The Soldier and the State* (Cambridge, MA: Harvard University Press, 1957), p. 69.

20. Sweeney is quoted in Robert S. McNamara, "Notes on October 21, 1962 Meeting with the President," October, 21, 1962, Cuban Missile Crisis 1962 Documents Collection, (Alexandria, VA: Chadwick-Healy, 1990), microfiche 1372-00738, p. 2. Moreover, the 90 percent success rate referred only to the thirty-six *known* missile sites; U.S. intelligence agencies estimated that there were four additional missile sites in Cuba that had not yet been found on October 21. *Ibid.*

21. Chronology of JCS Decisions Concerning the Cuban Crisis, Historical Division, Joint Chiefs of Staff, (Freedom of Information Act Request), p. 23 and p. 49. The latter recommendation was not unanimous: Chairman of the Joint Chiefs, General Maxwell Taylor, recommended against "taking the decision to execute now" and wanted instead to maintain a readiness to launch the air strike and invasion with a twelve-hour notice. *Ibid.*

22. Bernard Brodie, *War and Politics* (London: Cassel, 1974), p. 496.

23. See Roberta Wohlstetter, *Pearl Harbor: Warning and Decision* (Stanford, CA: Stanford University Press, 1962), pp. 10–11 and pp. 73–74; and Gordon W. Prange, *At Dawn We Slept* (New York: McGraw-Hill, 1991), pp. 411–12.

24. D. Clayton James, *The Years of MacArthur: Volume II, 1941–1945* (Boston: Houghton Mifflin, 1975), pp. 3–15 and Louis Morton, *The Fall of The Philippines* (Washington, DC: GPO, 1953), pp. 79–90.

25. R. V. Jones, *The Wizard's War: British Scientific Intelligence 1939–1945* (New York: Coward, McCann and Geoghegan, 1978), pp. 360–64; and Basil Collier, *The Battle of the V-Weapons, 1944–1945* (Morley, Yorkshire: Elmfield Press, 1976), pp. 23–41.

26. *The Military Balance* (London: International Institute for Strategic

Studies, 1991), p. 108.

27. Shamir speech of August 9 1990, as quoted in Shai Feldman, "Israeli Deterrence and the Gulf War," in Joseph Alpher, ed., *War in the Gulf* (Boulder, CO: Westview Press, 1992), p. 197.

28. See Paul Lewis, "U.N. Experts Now Say Baghdad Was Far from Making an A-bomb before Gulf War," *New York Times*, May 20, 1992, p. 6.

29. It certainly is possible that U.S. nuclear weapons deterred Saddam Hussein from using chemical weapons in 1991. It is also possible, however, that organizational problems, not deterrence, prevented their use: the Iraqis may have intended to move chemical weapons down to the battlefield once the war began, but the command and control and distribution system was severely disrupted by the U.S. offensive. See Rick Atkinson, "No Chemicals Found on Battlefields," *Washington Post*, March 7, 1991, p. A1.

30. See Sagan, *Moving Targets*, pp. 42–43. Problems in the development of meaningful limited options were not, moreover, solved by the changes Schlesinger made in war planning guidance and continued well into the late 1980s. For a very valuable analysis see Janne E. Nolan, *Guardians of the Arsenal: The Politics of Nuclear Strategy* (New York: Basic Books, 1989), pp. 248–61.

31. Atomic Energy Commission, Proposed Safety Rules for B-47 and B-52 Aircraft, August 1, 1960, p. 37 (Freedom of Information Act request) and B-52E/B-52 F Flight Manual, T.O. 1B-52E-1 (February 5, 1967, revised September 30, 1970), pp. 4–162.

32. See Theodore A. Postol, "Possible Fatalities from Superfires Following Nuclear Attacks in or Near Urban Areas," in Frederic Solomon and Robert Q. Marston, eds., *The Medical Implications of Nuclear War* (Washington: National Academy Press, 1986), pp. 15–72; and Lynn Eden, "Constructing Destruction: The Making of Organizational Knowledge of U.S. Nuclear Weapons Effects," (unpublished manuscript).

33. In addition, for a valuable analysis of the likelihood that similar organizational factors could have produced inadvertent escalation during a conventional war between the Warsaw Pact and NATO, see Barry R. Posen, *Inadvertent Escalation: Conventional War and Nuclear Risks* (Ithaca, NY: Cornell University Press, 1991).

34. See Jose Goldemberg and Harold A. Feiveson, "Denuclearization in Argentina and Brazil," *Arms Control Today* 24, no. 2 (March 1994), pp. 10–14.

35. See Albright, "South Africa's Secret Nuclear Weapons"; Darryl Howlett and John Simpson, "Nuclearisation and Denuclearisation in South Africa," *Survival* 35, no. 3 (Autumn 1993), pp. 154–73; and J. W. de Villers, Roger Jardine, and Mitchell Reiss, "Why South Africa Gave Up the Bomb," *Foreign Affairs* 72, no. 5 (November/December 1993), pp. 98–109.

36. McGeorge Bundy, William J. Crowe, Jr., and Sidney D. Drell, *Reducing Nuclear Danger* (New York: Council on Foreign Relations, 1993), pp. 81–85.

37. For imaginative studies see Roger D. Speed, *The International Control of Nuclear Weapons* (Stanford, CA: Center for International Security and Arms Control, 1994) and Regina Cowen Carp, ed., *Security without Nuclear Weapons* (Oxford: Oxford University Press, 1992).

INDEX

accidents, 75–78, 90, 96–99
  "bomb in basement" policy and, 121
  civilian-military relations and, 82, 123
  likelihood of, 118–23
  margin of error and, 82–83
  new nuclear states and, 80–81, 97–98, 119–22
  nuclear weapons safety and, 80–85
  organizational learning and, 123
  organization theory and, 75–78, 80–83, 113
  in post-Cold War world, 119
  proliferation and, 80–85
  theory of, 76–78
  tight coupling systems and, 82
  U.S. experience with, 78–80, 119
Acheson, Dean, 25
Air Force, U.S., 69, 70–71
Air War College, 59
Albright, David, 74
Algeria, viii, 85
Amin, Idi, 12
Anderson, Orvil, 59, 124
Angell, Norman, 45
Arab-Israeli conflict, 48
Arab-Israeli War (1973), 79, 122, 128
Argentina, 128–29, 133
arms races, 9
  deterrence and, 29–33
  first-strike capability and, 30–31
  flexible response policy and, 32
  force comparisons and, 30
  new nuclear states and, 31–32
Austria, 107
Ayub Khan, Mohammed, 62–63

Bajpai, Shankar, 41
Baker, James, 106
"balance of resolve," 25
balance of terror, 45
Ballistic Missile Early Warning System (BMEWS), 79–80
Beard, Edmund, 70
Begin, Menachem, 19
Belarus, vii, 49, 83, 122, 134
Bengal, 63
B-52 bomber, 79–80
Bhopal disaster, 118
Bhutto, Benazir, 41, 63, 82
blackmail, 15–16
Blair, Bruce, 96, 113, 119

BMEWS (Ballistic Missile Early Warning System), 79–80
"bomb in the basement" policy, 121
Bracken, Paul, 119
Bradley, Omar, 102
Brazil, 133
Brecht, Bertolt, 93
Brezhnev, Leonid, 25
Brodie, Bernard, 6, 24, 108, 126
Brown, Harold, 30, 31, 34
Bueno de Mesquita, Bruce, 47–48
Bundy, McGeorge, 135
Bush, George, 97, 103–4
Butler, George Lee, 40

Carter, Jimmy, 97
Central Intelligence Agency (CIA), vii, 38, 41, 43, 82, 123
Challenger accident, 118
Cheney, Richard, 106
Chernobyl disaster, 118
China, Nationalist, 7
China, People's Republic of, 17, 31, 38, 39, 40, 41, 44, 62, 122
  civilian-military relations in, 14
  Cultural Revolution in, 10, 71–72, 85
  Korean War and, 15–16, 57–58
  nuclear forces of, 39, 42, 65–66, 127
  Soviet Union and, 11, 20, 21–22, 42, 45, 75, 106
  strategic weapons deployment of, 71–72
CIA (Central Intelligence Agency), vii, 38, 41, 43, 82, 123
civilian-military relations, 123–26
  accidents and, 82, 123
  budget limits and, 99–100
  in China, 14
  Cold War and, 57–58, 131–32
  deterrence and, 14–15, 49, 88–90
  Eisenhower and, 99–100
  Gulf War and, 104, 106–7
  military's conservatism and, 102–3, 107–8
  organization theory and, 70, 82, 88–89
  preventive war and, 57–58, 103–5, 124–25
  proliferation and, 86
  in Russia, 65–66
  in Soviet Union, 99–101

civilian-military relations (*continued*)
　U.S. and, 99–101
　war and, 56–57
Clinton, Bill, 130
Cold War, 38, 86, 103, 116
　civilian-military relations and, 57–
　　58, 131–32
　nuclear near-accidents in, 78–80
　nuclear war and, 41
　risk of accidents in, 118–19
　U.S.-Soviet relations in, 14, 17, 20,
　　23, 25, 42–43, 47, 65, 67, 75, 82–
　　83, 109, 123, 124, 131
Cominform, 59
"Coming National Crisis, The"
　(Twining), 60
Congress, U.S., 69, 100, 109
　House of Representatives, 43
　Senate, 25, 43, 100
counterforce, 100, 132
countervalue, 100
credibility, 22–26, 27
Crimean War, 5, 101–2
Crowe, William, 135
Cuban missile crisis, 5, 110
　near-accident during, 78–79, 111
　organization theory and, 74
Cultural Revolution, 10, 71–72, 85
culture of reliability, 76
Czechoslovakia, 28, 107

"decapitation" attack, 121
decolonization, 2
defense:
　ideal, 3–4
　military organizations and, 49
　second-strike force and, 4
Defense Department, U.S., 100–101,
　102
"defensive last resort" doctrine, 135
de Klerk, F. W., 133
Desert Storm, Operation, vii
deterrence:
　arms races and, 29–33
　"balance of resolve" and, 25
　balance of terror and, 45
　basic strategy of, 3–4
　blackmail threat and, 15–16
　capabilities and, 6
　civilian-military relations and, 14–
　　15, 49, 88–90
　credibility and, 22–26, 27
　extended, 26–29
　first-strike capability and, 30–31
　flexible response policy and, 32
　"generic targetting" and, 40
　hostile pairs and, 14, 40–41
　intensity of war and, 33–37
　irrational rulers and, 12–13, 97–98

Killian Report and, 109–10
Korean situation and, 37–39
massive retaliation and, 16
miscalculation and, 6–7
mutual devastation and, 23
Nazi Germany and, 28–29
nuclear war strategy and, 98–99
organization theory compared
　with, 50–55
preventive vs. preemptive strikes
　and, 17–19
radical, or rogue states, and, 11–
　12, 39–40, 97
"rational deterrence theory" and,
　50–55, 86, 112,–13
requirements of, 20–22, 30, 51, 54
second-strike force and, 4, 23, 25,
　27, 32–33, 51, 66–67, 108–10, 116
by small nuclear force, 17–19
structural theory and, 112
territory and, 5–6, 26
Third World and, 13
uncertainty and, 108, 110–11, 128–
　29
unstable societies and, 12–13
U.S.-Soviet relations and, 23, 25,
　26, 36, 42, 45
war and, 5, 36–37
war fighting compared with, 30–31
Dien Bien Phu, battle of, 16
domestic stability, 8–10, 49, 84–85
Dreadnought, 6
Drell, Sidney, 135
Dulles, John Foster, 15–16, 26

Egypt, 12, 13, 73, 127, 128
Eisenhower, Dwight D., 15, 30, 60–
　62, 70, 109
　control of military and, 99–100
　preventive war idea rejected by, 61
Eisenhower administration, 58, 59,
　101
Erlanger, Steven, 112
ethnocentrism, 115
extended deterrence, 26–29

Falkland War, 128–29
Feaver, Peter, 119
Feldman, Shai, 12, 48
first-strike capability, 30–31
flexible-response policy, 32
foreign policy, 11–12
Forrestal, James, 99
Fox, William T. R., 30
France, 37, 43, 122
　Crimean War and, 5, 101–2
　deterrent force of, 31
　Indochina and, 16
　Soviet Union and, 14, 17, 31

France *(continued)*
 World War I and, 6–7
 World War II and, 28, 107
Franco, Francisco, 98
French, David T., 38
F-16 aircraft, 82

Galen, Justin (pseud.), 22
"generic targetting," 40
Georgia, 65
Germany, Federal Republic of (West
 Germany), 32
Germany, Imperial, 6
Germany, Nazi, 7, 39, 98, 107, 127
 nuclear deterrence and, 28–29
Germany, reunified, 48
Giscard d'Estaing, Val,ry, 31
goal displacement, 53
Great Britain, 12, 28, 37, 43
 Crimean War and, 5, 101–2
 Falklands War and, 128–29
 Soviet Union and, 14, 17, 31, 109
 V-1 buzz bomb and, 127–28
 World War II and, 7, 107
Greenland, 119
Grenada, 102
Gulf War, *see* Persian Gulf War

Haiti, 102
Hanami, Andrew, 38
Helms, Richard, 43
Hiroshima bombing, 19
Hitler, Adolf, 28–29, 39, 107
Ho Chi Minh, 16
hostile pairs, 14, 40–41
House of Representatives, U.S., 43
Hungary, 26
Hussein, Saddam, 13, 40, 97, 104,
 129–30

ICBM, *see* intercontinental ballistic
 missile
Ignalina nuclear plant, 84
India, 38, 40, 48, 121
 Kashmir crisis and, 122
 nuclear program of, 31, 43, 81
 Pakistan's conflict with, 41, 62–63,
 82–83, 112
interactive complexity, 76
intercontinental ballistic missiles
 (ICBM), 68–71, 72, 100
 airborne alert system and, 79–80
 hair-trigger forces and, 96–97
International Atomic Energy
 Agency, 40
international relations theory, 86–88,
 112–13, 136
invulnerable forces concept, 71–74
Iran, viii, 16

Iraq, vii, 38, 40, 110–11, 121, 123
 Israel's strike against reactor in,
 17–19, 106
 nuclear program of, 38, 40, 81,
 110–11, 119, 129–30
 SCUD missiles launched by, 13,
 129–30
Israel, 21, 28, 37, 95, 111, 122, 128
 deterrent logic and, 33
 Egyptian air force destroyed by,
 73, 127
 Iraqi reactor destroyed by, 17–19,
 106
 nuclear program of, 31, 40, 81
 SCUD missiles launched against,
 13, 129–30
Italy, 98

Japan, vii, 7, 38, 40, 48, 102, 127
Jericho missiles, 122, 129
Jervis, Robert, 4
JL-1 program, 72
Johnson, Lyndon B., 43
Johnson administration, 100–101
Joint Chiefs of Staff, 25, 54, 99, 100,
 131
 preventive war and, 58, 59–61,
 124, 125

Kashmir crisis, 82, 122
Kazakhstan, vii, 49, 83, 122, 134
Kemp, Geoffrey, 22
Kendall, Henry, 96, 113
Kennan, George, 86–87
Kennedy, John F., 5, 32, 100, 111
Kennedy administration, 100–101
Kenney, George, 59
Khrushchev, Nikita, 5, 111
Killian Committee, 70, 109–10
Kim Il Sung, 39, 97
Kissinger, Henry, 25
Kohn, Richard H., 102–3
Korea, People's Republic of (North
 Korea), vii, 25, 82–83, 110, 123,
 127
 deterrence and, 37–39
 nuclear weapons program of, 37–
 39, 40, 41, 73–74, 81, 134
 South Korea contrasted with, 38–
 39
 U.S. and, 37, 39–40
Korea, Republic of (South Korea),
 16, 82–83, 110
 North Korea contrasted with, 38–
 39
Korean War, 15–16, 102
 "balance of resolve" and, 25
 Chinese intervention in, 57–58
Kutuzov, Mikhail, 101
Kuwait, 13, 104, 106, 111, 129

Laird, Melvin, 101
launch-on-warning policy, 113
Lavoy, Peter, 48
Lebanon, 102
LeMay, Curtis, 59, 70, 124
Libya, viii, 12, 21, 129
Limits of Safety, The (Sagan), 76–77
Lithuania, 84

McArthur, Douglas, 25, 102
McCain, John, 39
McNamara, Robert S., 32, 34, 100,
    109, 131–32, 133
    "unacceptable damage" defined
    by, 21
McNarney, General, 99
Maginot Line, 4
Manchuria, 102
Mao Zedong, 72, 127
March, James, 53
Marshall, George C., 102
Maslin, Yevgeny, 83
massive retaliation, 16
Matthews, Francis P., 17, 58
Mearsheimer, John, 48, 64
Middle East, 48
military:
    conservatism of, 102–3, 107–8, 109,
    124
    Eisenhower and, 99–100
    organization theory and, 48–49,
    53–54, 67–68
    preventive war and, 56–57, 124–26
    war and, 56–57, 107
    see also civilian-military relations
Minuteman missile, 79, 96
missile gap crisis, 70
Morgan, Patrick, 34
Morgenthau, Hans, 86–87
Moroccan crises, 102
Mother Courage (Brecht), 93

NASA, 118
Nasser, Gamal, 18, 73
National Security Council (NSC), 60–
    61
    NSC-68 of, 58
NATO (North Atlantic Treaty
    Organization), 26, 35
Navy, U.S., 69–70, 96
    Polaris program and, 69–70, 109
"New Look" defense policy, 101
New York Times, 112
Nie Rongzhen, 85
Nixon, Richard M., 101
Non-Proliferation Treaty, 38, 40, 43,
    74, 134–35
Normal Accidents (Perrow), 76
normal accident theory, 76–78

North American Air Defense
    Command (NORAD), 79, 80
North Atlantic Treaty Organization
    (NATO), 26, 35
NSC (National Security Council), 60–
    61
    NSC-68 of, 58
nuclear development, 18
nuclear-free zone, 133

organization theory:
    accidents and, 75–78, 80–83
    civilian-military relations and, 70,
    82, 88–89
    counter-proliferation policy and,
    88–91
    Cuban missile crisis and, 74
    culture of reliability and, 76
    domestic stability and, 84–85
    goals and, 53
    interactive complexity and, 76
    international relations theory and,
    86–88, 136
    invulnerable forces concept and,
    71–74
    military and, 48–49, 53–54, 67–68
    new nuclear states and, 71–75, 80–
    81
    normal accidents theory and, 76–
    77
    politics of blame and, 77
    proliferation and, 75–78, 88–89
    rational deterrence theory
    compared with, 50–55, 112–13
    redundant systems and, 77
    routinized behavior and, 74, 97–98
    strategic weapons deployment
    and, 71–73
    survivable forces and, 66–68, 71–75
    tight coupling systems and, 76,
    82–83
    U.S. case and, 54–55, 68–71

Pakistan, 38, 40, 48, 121
    India's conflict with, 41, 62–63, 82–
    83, 112
    Kashmir crisis and, 82, 122
    nuclear program of, 41, 43, 81
Panama, 103–4
Pearl Harbor attack, 127
People's Liberation Army, Chinese,
    72
permissive action links (PALS), 96
Perrow, Charles, 53, 76
Persian Gulf War, vii, 40, 81, 104,
    110–11, 121, 122
    civilian-military relations and, 104,
    106–7
    SCUD missiles in, 13, 129–30

Philippines, 127
Poland, 28, 107
Polaris missile system, 69–70, 109
Politburo, 14, 65
Posen, Barry, 48, 64–65
Powell, Colin, 102
Power, Thomas, 59, 124
preventive war:
  advocates of, 124
  China's nuclear arsenal and, 65–66
  civilian-military relations and, 57–58, 103–5, 124–25
  Eisenhower's rejection of, 61
  JCS and, 58, 59–61, 124, 125
  military as advocate of, 56–57, 124–26
  new nuclear states and, 61–66
  NSC-68 and, 58
  organization theory and, 75–78, 88–89
  Pakistan-India conflict and, 62–63
  preemptive strikes and, 17–19
  Project Control study and, 59
  Russia-Ukraine relations and, 63–65
  with Soviet Union, 58–59
  survivability and, 68
  transition period and, 55–57
  Twining memorandum on, 60
  U.S. case and, 57–61
proliferation, 1
  accidents and, 80–85
  civilian-military relations and, 86
  conventional weapons, 112
  covert nature of, 81
  efforts against, 133–34
  managing of, 89–91
  nuclear weapons safety and, 80–85
  organization theory and, 75–78, 88–89
see also specific topics

Qaddafi, Muammar el-, 12, 97
Quarles, Donald A., 30

Radford, Arthur, 59–61, 124
RAND Corporation, 69
rationality, 24, 50–55, 85–86, 87, 113
regional stability, 10–17
  foreign policy and, 11–12
  new vs. old nuclear powers and, 11
Rhineland, 28
Rickover, Hyman, 109
Riker, William, 47–48
Rose, Leo, 63
Rosen, Steven J., 28
Russell, Bertrand, 58
Russia, Imperial, 5, 101–2
Russia, post-Soviet:
  civilian-military relations and, 65–66
  post-Cold War nuclear safety and, 90–91, 94, 119
  Ukraine and, 48, 63–65, 82–83, 112, 134
  see also Soviet Union

SAC, *see* Strategic Air Command
Sadat, Anwar, 12
Sapolsky, Harvey, 69–70
Schelling, Thomas, 24, 34
Schlesinger, James, 132
Schwarzkopf, Norman, 106–7
SCUD missile, 129
Second Artillery Division, Chinese, 72
second-strike forces, 68, 71, 75, 123
  defense and, 4
  deterrence and, 4, 23, 25, 27, 32–33, 51, 66–67, 108–10, 116
  organization theory and, 66–67
  weak nuclear states and, 17–25, 108–10, 126–28
security, 42–44
self-help systems, 2–8
  anarchy and, 3
  security and, 3
Senate, U.S., 100
  Foreign Relations Committee of, 25, 43
Shalikashvili, John, 130
Shamir, Yitzhak, 129
Siberia, 111
Siegfried Line, 107
Simmel, Georg, 6
Simon, Herbert, 53
Sino-Soviet alliance, 59
Sisson, Richard, 63
SLBM (submarine launched ballistic missile), 68–71, 72
Smith, Bruce, 69
Smoke, Richard, 34
Snow, C. P., 93, 96
Snyder, Glenn, 25
South Africa, vii, 123
  nuclear program of, 81, 120, 133–34
Soviet Union, 7, 19, 28, 38, 39, 40, 61, 98
  "born nuclear" states of former, vii, 1, 49, 84–85, 94, 122
  China and, 11, 20, 21–22, 42, 45, 75, 106
  civilian-military relations and, 99–101
  France and, 14, 17, 31
  Great Britain and, 14, 17, 31, 109
  Hungarian Revolution and, 26

Soviet Union *(continued)*
  Korean War and, 15–16
  Politburo of, 14, 65
  preventive attack on, 58–59
  U.S.'s Cold War relations with, 14,
    17, 20, 23, 25, 42–43, 47, 65, 67,
    75, 82–83, 109, 123, 124, 131
  World War II and, 34–35
  see Russia, post-Soviet
Spain, 98
special weapons emergency
    separation system (SWESS), 132
spread of nuclear weapons, 1–2, 8,
    37–41, 42, 47–48, 93, 94, 112,
    133–35
stability:
  domestic, 8–10, 49, 84–85
  regional, 10–17
Stalin, Joseph, 39
State Department, U.S., 59–60, 102
Strategic Air Command (SAC), 69,
    70, 78
  monitor mission of, 79–80
  SWESS system of, 132
strategic bombing, 68–71, 72
submarine launched ballistic missile
    (SLBM), 68–71, 72
Sudetenland, 107
survivable forces:
  new nuclear states and, 17–25, 71–
    75, 108–10
  organization theory and, 66–68,
    71–75
Sweeney, Walter, 124–25
SWESS (special weapons emergency
    separation system), 132
Syria, 13, 128

Tactical Air Command, U.S., 110,
    124
Taiwan, 25
Tartarstan, 83
"Team Spirit" exercises, 40
territory, 5–6
terrorists, 19, 40, 94–96
Theory of International Politics (Waltz),
    87
Third World, 13, 40, 51, 97
Three Mile Island accident, 118
tight coupling systems, 76, 82–83
Transdniestr Republic, 65
Trident missile, 119
Truman, Harry S., 17, 57, 58, 59, 62,
    99
Truman administration, 58
Twining, Nathan, 59, 60, 124

Ukraine, vii, 49, 112, 122
  nuclear safety in, 83

Russia and, 48, 63–65, 82–83, 134
"unacceptable damage," 21, 25, 51
uncertainty, 15, 108, 110–11, 128–29
United Nations, 38, 81
United States:
  civilian-military relations and, 99–
    101
  new nuclear states and, 89–91,
    122, 134–35
  North Korea's nuclear program
    and, 37, 39–40
  nuclear safety and, 78–80, 119
  organization theory and, 54–55,
    68–71
  Soviet Union's Cold War relations
    with, 14, 17, 20, 23, 25, 42–43,
    47, 65, 67, 75, 82–83, 109, 123,
    124, 131
U-2 aircraft, 111

Vagts, Alfred, 101
van Creveld, Martin, 48
Vandenberg, Hoyt, 59, 124
Van Evera, Stephen, 48
Vietnam War, 101
V-1 buzz bomb, 127–28
Von Neumann, John, 58

war, 2, 4
  civilian-military relations and, 56–
    57
  conventional, 7–8, 45
  deterrence and, 5, 36–37
  domestic stability and, 8–10
  expected costs of, 5
  frequency and intensity of, 33–37
  military organizations and, 56–57,
    107
  nuclear, 7–8
  relative strengths and, 6
  uncertainty and, 15, 108
  between U.S. and Soviet Union,
    35–36, 131–33
  Weinberger Doctrine and, 102
Warnke, Paul, 34
Weinberger, Caspar, 102
White, Thomas, 59, 124
Wiesner, Jerome, 100
Woolsey, James, 41
World War I, 6–7
World War II, 2, 6, 7, 36, 69, 98, 102,
    107
  France and, 14, 17, 31
  Great Britain and, 14, 17, 31, 109
  nuclear weapons and, 28–29
  Soviet Union and, 34–35
  V-1 buzz bomb and, 127–28

Yeltsin, Boris, 64, 65
York, Herbert, 109

UNITED
KINGDOM

FRANCE

ALG

UNITED STATES

BRAZIL

ARGENTINA

The Spread of Nuclear Weapons: 1945 to the Pres

Declared Nuclear Weapons States

Newly Independent States with Nuclear Weapons on Terri
Belarus, Kazakhstan, and Ukraine have acceded to the Non-Prolifer
Treaty as non-nuclear weapons states. All are transferring nuclear
weapons to Russia.

Undeclared Nuclear Weapons States These nations are belie
to be able to deploy one or more nuclear weapons rapidly or to ha
deployed them already.

Active/Suspected Nuclear Weapons Programs North Kore
Iran, and Libya have taken steps in the past several years to acquire
nuclear weapons capabilities. Algeria may also have done so.

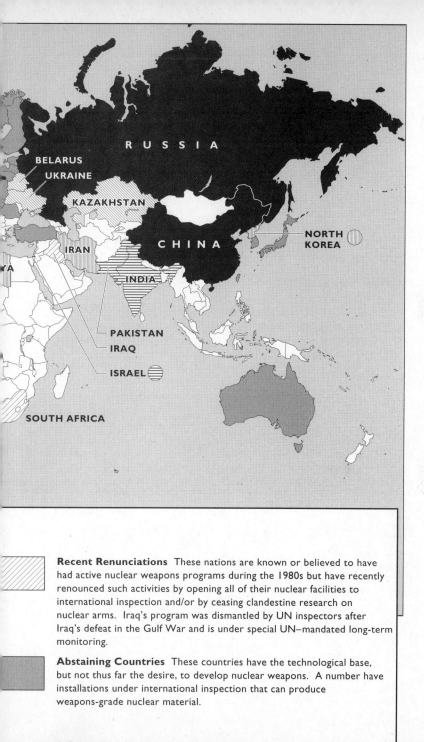

Recent Renunciations These nations are known or believed to have had active nuclear weapons programs during the 1980s but have recently renounced such activities by opening all of their nuclear facilities to international inspection and/or by ceasing clandestine research on nuclear arms. Iraq's program was dismantled by UN inspectors after Iraq's defeat in the Gulf War and is under special UN–mandated long-term monitoring.

Abstaining Countries These countries have the technological base, but not thus far the desire, to develop nuclear weapons. A number have installations under international inspection that can produce weapons-grade nuclear material.